GOD UP THERE?

A Study in
DIVINE TRANSCENDENCE

By

DAVID CAIRNS

THE SAINT ANDREW PRESS
EDINBURGH

First published in 1967
by the Saint Andrew Press
121 George Street, Edinburgh 2

To

RALPH AND JENNY MORTON

in gratitude for a long friendship.

I wish also to express my thanks to the Council for the Cunningham Lectureship, who invited me to give the Lectures, to the Students of New College, Edinburgh, who listened to them, and discussed them with me, to the Editor of the *Expository Times*, for permission to use published material in Chapter V, and not least to the Rev. and Mrs. Robin Barbour, my kind hosts during the weeks when the Lectures were being delivered.

DAVID CAIRNS

CHRIST'S COLLEGE, ABERDEEN
    October 1967.

Printed in Great Britain
by T. and A. CONSTABLE LTD., Hopetoun Street
Printers to the University of Edinburgh.

CONTENTS

LIST OF BOOKS

Quoted or mentioned in the text: arranged in alphabetical order according to the names of the authors, together with titles as cited in the text

JOHN BAILLIE
    Our Knowledge of God. Oxford (1939).

KARL BARTH
    The Humanity of God. John Knox Press, Richmond, Va. (1960).

    Originally published in German as three separate monographs in the *Theologische Studien* series, by Evangelischer Verlag A.G. Zollikon, Zürich (1953-7).

DIETRICH BONHOEFFER
    Widerstand und Ergebung. Chr. Kaiser Verlag, München (1951).

    E.T. *Letters and Papers from Prison.* S.C.M. Press, London (1953).

EMIL BRUNNER
    Erlebnis, Erkenntnis, und Glaube. J. C. B. Mohr, Tübingen (1921).

    Philosophie und Offenbarung. J. C. B. Mohr, Tübingen (1925).

    Das Gebot und die Ordnungen. J. C. B. Mohr, Tübingen (1932).

    E.T. *The Divine Imperative.* Lutterworth Press, London (1937).

    Mensch im Widerspruch. Furche Verlag, Berlin (1937).

    E.T. *Man in Revolt.* Lutterworth Press, London (1939).

    Offenbarung und Vernunft. Zwingli Verlag, Zürich (1943).

    E.T. *Revelation and Reason.* Lutterworth Press, London (1947).

    Dogmatik I. Die Christliche Lehre von Gott. Zwingli Verlag, Zürich (1946).

EMIL BRUNNER
  E.T. *The Christian Doctrine of God.* Vol. I. Lutterworth,
  London (1949). Cited as *Dogmatik I.*
  Wahrleit als Begegnung, 2nd Edn., Zwingli Verlag, Zürich
  (1963).
  E.T. *Truth as Encounter*, 2nd Edn. S.C.M. Press, London
  (1964).

EDWARD FARLEY
  The Transcendence of God. Westminster Press, Philadelphia
  (1960).

HELMUT GOLLWITZER
  Die Existenz Gottes im Bekenntnis des Glaubens. Chr. Kaiser
  Verlag, München (1963).
  E.T. *The Existence of God as Confessed by Faith.* S.C.M.
  Press, London (1965). Cited as *Existenz Gottes.*

HELMUT GOLLWITZER AND HERBERT BRAUN
  Post Bultmann Locutum; eine Diskussion. Herbert Reich,
  Evangelischer Verlag, Hamburg-Bergstedt (1965).

KENNETH HAMILTON
  The System and the Gospel. S.C.M. Press, London (1965).
  Revolt against Heaven. Eerdmans, Grand Rapids (1965).
  God is Dead; the Anatomy of a Slogan. Eerdmans (1966).
  Cited as *God is Dead.*

H. J. IWAND
  Glauben und Wissen. Chr. Kaiser Verlag, München (1962).

DAVID JENKINS
  Guide to the Debate about God. Lutterworth Press, London
  (1966).

EBERHARD JÜNGEL
  Gottes Sein ist im Werden. J. C. B. Mohr (Paul Siebeck),
  Tübingen (1965).

HENDRIK KRAEMER
  The Christian Message in a non-Christian World. Lutterworth, London (1938).
  Religion and the Christian Faith. Lutterworth, London
  (1956).

C. KEGLEY
>The Theology of Emil Brunner. Macmillan, London (1962).

ERIC MASCALL
>The Secularisation of Christianity. Darton Longman and Todd, London (1965).

JOHN MORRISON
>Honesty and God. Saint Andrew Press, Edinburgh (1966).

THOMAS OGLETREE
>The Death of God Controversy. S.C.M. Press, London (1966).

WERNER AND LOTTE PELZ
>God is no More. Gollancz, London (1964).

J. A. T. ROBINSON
>Honest to God. S.C.M. Press, London (1963).
>The New Reformation? S.C.M. Press, London (1965).

ROBINSON AND DAVID EDWARDS
>The Honest to God Debate. S.C.M. Press, London (1963).

ROMAN ROESSLER
>Person und Glaube: Der Personalismus der Gottesbeziehung bei Emil Brunner. Christian Kaiser Verlag, München (1965).

R. GREGOR SMITH
>The New Man. S.C.M. Press, London (1956).
>Secular Christianity. Collins, London (1966).

PAUL TILLICH
>The Protestant Era. Nisbet, London (1951).
>Systematic Theology. Vol. I. Nisbet, London (1953).
>Systematic Theology. Vol. II. Nisbet, London (1957).
>Biblical Religion and the Search for Ultimate Reality. Nisbet, London (1955). Cited as Biblical Religion.

PAUL VAN BUREN
>The Secular Meaning of the Gospel. S.C.M. Press, London (1963).

COLIN WILLIAMS
>Where in the World. Epworth, London (1965).
>What in the World. Epworth, London (1965).
>Faith in a Secular Age. Collins, London, Fontana Books (1966).

Note by the Author

Though I have done my best to provide page references in the English editions of books originally published in German, the reader will find that the passages quoted by me do not exactly tally with the published English translations. The reason for this is that, where possible, I prefer to make my own translations from the German originals.

CHAPTER I

The Present Predicament: Diagnoses and Prescriptions

THERE have been times in the history of Christian thought when it seemed as if the solid earth had moved beneath men's feet. This has happened once again today, and it is time to re-examine our theological foundations to see whether they have cracked, and are in need of regrouting. Such an examination is now in progress, and this book is intended as a small contribution to it. In earthquakes there is usually one main centre or line of shock, and in this day of the shaking of the theological foundations it is not hard to say in what area the tremors have occurred. They have been felt in relation to the doctrine of God's transcendence.

And yet this picture of regrouting is far too negative to describe the present situation, as if we were merely filling up unsightly cracks in a temple, or shoring up some tottering Dagon. The Lord has caused the earthquake, or at least he is in it, and therefore this is a time not only of confusion but of tremendous promise. It may be that we are in sight of a new Reformation. But if so, it would be tragic if we were unable to benefit by it because theological confusion had made us powerless.

We shall later need to examine the writings of a number of men more closely, but one or two striking quotations from theologians of today may help to enforce my point about the contemporary situation. In his book *Guide to the Debate about God*, David Jenkins opens with a chapter called, with a question-mark, "The Beginning of the End?" Jenkins asks whether the present debate, sparked off in this country by John Robinson's *Honest to God*, is "simply a recurring phenomenon which has to be reckoned with as a normal feature in the life of man in the world, and of his dealings with and soundings after God? Or does the form which the debate is taking this time show that it is really a decisively heightened crisis of a wasting disease?" (p. 9). I shall later in this chapter have to deal with Jenkins's own diagnosis and prescription, but press on now to give one or two more quotations from other writers to illustrate my point.

In Colin William's little book *Faith in a Secular Age* there is a passage called "Transcendence" (pp. 75-88), which Edwin Robertson in *The British Weekly* described as "Thirteen superb pages on Transcendence". The interesting point here is that Williams writes the whole passage with hardly a reference to God. In these pages the concept of God seems to me not to be so much merely absent as consciously suppressed. While making this criticism I would like to pay tribute to Williams's two previous books, *Where in the World* and *What in the World*, which are quite exceptionally interesting and stimulating.

Further to the theological left we have a few sentences from a comparatively moderate exponent of the new radicalism, the Bishop of Woolwich, who demands, in the preface to his book, *Honest to God*, a very thorough recasting of our theology. While appreciating the work of those theologians who "see the best, and indeed the only defence of doctrine to be in the firm reiteration, in fresh and intelligent contemporary language, of 'the faith once delivered to the saints' "—Dr. Robinson goes on to say, "At the same time, I believe that we are being called, over the years ahead, to far more than a restating of traditional orthodoxy in modern terms. Indeed, if our defence of the faith is limited to this, we shall find, in all likelihood, that we have lost out to all but a very tiny religious remnant. . . . A much more radical recasting, I would judge, is demanded, in the process of which the most fundamental categories in our theology, of God, of the supernatural, and of religion itself, must go into the melting-pot."[1]

Much further to the left we have Werner Pelz's book, *God is no More*, which attempts to interpret the life and

[1] *Honest to God*, p. 7.

mission of Jesus without bringing in God the Father at all. "There is no God but Jesus, says the author of St. John's Gospel, because his words more than any other words, build us up, refresh us, guide and gather us, resuscitate us, because they bring us life and the abundance of it. . . ."[1] His saying, for which he paid with his life, namely that he and the Father are one, "did not mean what it has hitherto been thought to mean, but that his hope was his God. In so far as he lived his hope, he had the right to say: I and my hope are one. He who has seen me has seen my hope. . . . He who has seen me has seen God."[2] Here we have an attempt to create a gospel without God, and while Pelz makes no attempt to justify this strange project, the very fact that he can call his book *God is no More* and proceed quietly on the assumption that his thesis requires no preliminary vindication, is itself a strong sign of the contemporary mood.

Representing a rather similar view we have Paul van Buren, who, unlike Pelz, does give us grounds for the position he takes up. It is from the standpoint of the radical linguistic philosophy that he declares that the word "God" is meaningless. "The empiricist in us finds the heart of the difficulty not in what is said about God, but in the very talking about God at all. We do not know 'what' God is, and we cannot understand how the word 'God' is being used."[3] The result here is like that which we found in Pelz. Later, Van Buren gives us an exegesis of John 14:8. "One of the disciples had asked Jesus to 'show' them the Father, as though something were still lacking in what Jesus has 'shown' them until that time. Jesus answers, 'Have I been with you so long, and yet you do not know me, Philip? He who has seen me has seen the Father; how can you say "Show us the Father"? Do you not believe that I am in the Father, and the Father in me?' "

Van Buren goes on to comment that "Father" is the word which Jesus apparently used frequently in cases where his contemporaries might have used the word 'God'. The further

---

[1] *God is no More*, p. 56.   [2] *Op. cit.*, p. 109.
[3] *The Secular Meaning of the Gospel*, p. 84.

explication of this word, however, is not the only, and not even the best, way to understand this passage, for the passage itself suggests a *via negativa* of an odd sort. The author asks us to stop "looking for the 'Father' " for we shall not find him, and the quest is beside the point in any case. So far van Buren.[1] In fact, that is precisely what the author of the Gospel does not tell us to do; he tells us where to look for the Father, for we shall find him in Jesus.

When the understanding of transcendence has either been endangered, or lost, as in these two last cases, it is obvious that further careful examination and inquiry is needed.

There is, indeed, as I have hinted, no fundamental unity among these men of the left. Robinson continues to believe in the living God, and claims that he can do justice to God's transcendence while discarding what he calls "supranaturalism". Pelz proclaims that God is no more. T. J. J. Altizer avers that the death of God is a historical event, and succeeds in explaining fairly clearly what he means. William Hamilton makes the same assertion, but has so far not been able to make his meaning clear. Van Buren, on the basis of the linguistic philosophy, claims that the concept "God" is without meaning. Yet for all this variety and confusion there is a tendency which all these writers share, which makes it legitimate for our purpose to group them together. And, before going further, we must express some indebtedness to these men of the left, even though sometimes feeling angry with them, and realising that some of them may rightly feel discomfort at the theological company they are keeping. We must be grateful to them, for they have not only aroused fears, irritation and even exasperation, but they have re-awakened interest in theology, and they have started a discussion whose final result must surely be for good.

So much, for the moment, for the literature of the left. We have now to take stock for a moment of the increasing volume of the literature of critical valuation and response. Outstanding on this side are books giving a considerable amount of detailed

[1] *Op. cit.*, p. 146.

criticism of the new writing. Of importance here is Professor Eric Mascall's book, *The Secularisation of Christianity*, which has brought van Buren's *The Secular Meaning of the Gospel* under the magnifying glass, and submitted Bishop Robinson's *Honest to God* to a detailed and annihilating critique which it would be tedious to attempt to rival. Helmut Gollwitzer has carried on the debate, principally with Herbert Braun, both in his book *Die Existenz Gottes im Bekenntnis des Glaubens* and in public debate (see *Post Bultmann Locutum*, Vols. I and II). He has also dealt more briefly with Rudolf Bultmann and Tillich, while Kenneth Hamilton in his books *Revolt against Heaven* and *God is Dead; the Anatomy of a Slogan* has given most valuable reports and criticisms, particularly of William Hamilton, T. J. J. Altizer and Gabriel Vahanian. A generous and perceptive critical study of these same men has appeared more recently, by Thomas Ogletree, *The Death of God Controversy*, while John Morrison has published a study of Robinson's first book.

It would be unprofitable to go once more over the ground covered so thoroughly by these critics. The theme of the present study is the transcendence of God, and reference will be made to the various writers of the right and the left only in so far as criticism and quotation can help towards this end. It is clear that a better understanding of the divine transcendence should be the chief aim of all constructive criticism of the new writing. For genuine criticism, while it may start destructively, inevitably moves forward into a more constructive phase. Questions are first asked about the real meaning of the new writers, and an attempt may be made to point out incoherencies and contradictions in their material, and to expose inadequate presuppositions and false alternatives underlying their expositions. But an effort must also be made to assimilate positive contributions by them, and to appreciate true concerns which they have felt, and it may be that attempts will be made to restate doctrines to which it is felt that they have done insufficient justice, or which their criticisms have shown to be vulnerable. Perhaps Professor Helmut Gollwitzer's important book *The Existence of God as Confessed by Faith* goes as far as any in this direction of reconstruction.

There is a further aspect of this critical and constructive response which is to be found in the serious attempts to evaluate the projects of the radical left. It is an attempt to understand the significance of this whole movement in the light of the theological past. It will be pretty generally agreed within the Church that the "Death of God" theologies are a somewhat hectic aberrant in its life. But surely they are symptomatic of a more deep-seated malady, not in God, but in the thought of the Church. And if this is so, then we have a clear duty to look at the patient's case-history, to try to find out what the causes of the illness have been. It is interesting, and indeed tantalising, to find that the specialists have made what appear to be two radically different diagnoses, and I shall in the next paragraphs attempt to set these forth in some more detail. It may be that in the end we shall find out that there is some truth on both sides, and that after all the diagnoses are not so completely contradictory as they at first appeared to be.

In order that the reader may have understanding of the next part of this chapter, its main thesis may be summarized as follows. There are some who declare that the patient is sick because he has been fed on a diet of pure transcendence, and cannot assimilate this. What he needs to help him are certain vitamins of natural theology. The opposing party declare that the reverse is the truth. The wasting disease is due to the poisons of natural theology, which have prevented the patient from assimilating the revelation of the transcendent God. It is not that God is dead, but that the patient is for the moment unable to assimilate the nurture of faith given in revelation.

It will now be necessary to develop these two opposing arguments in some detail with documentation. First, the argument of the exponents of natural theology. David Jenkins's book *Guide to the Debate about God* has a first chapter (which I have already mentioned) entitled, with a question-mark,

"The Beginning of the End of Theism?" He then goes on to expound the teaching of a list of Christian theologians, the first of whom, Joseph Butler, is an Englishman, while all the others are Protestant, German-speaking theologians. Bishop Butler's *Analogy of Religion*, Jenkins tells us, "represents a method of apology and argument which goes right back into the Christian tradition", and which, he himself thinks, "must, in however changed a form, have its equivalent today", while Schleiermacher (whose name heads the group that follows) "can reasonably be regarded as the innovator of a modern form of apologetics, and he certainly has had a great influence, whether by action or reaction, on the theologians we are to consider".[1]

The rest of the book is given up to a study of these theologians. After Schleiermacher come Rudolf Bultmann, Karl Barth, Emil Brunner, Paul Tillich and Dietrich Bonhoeffer. Jenkins's argument seeks to show that for all their differences from Schleiermacher, most of these theologians must for our purposes be grouped together with him as representing a false line in theology, a line antipathetic to a rational natural theology.

Butler divided his *Analogy* into two parts, the first being entitled "Of Natural Religion", and the second "Of Revealed Religion". Jenkins says of Butler, ". . . he holds that it is possible by directing the attention of reasonable men to reasonable arguments relating to the nature of the world, the nature of men, and the nature of men's life in the world, to show that something may be discovered and known about the existence of God, and even to some extent about His nature. . . . This is the normal pattern of Christian apologetic, worked out in its most classical form in the Middle Ages by Thomas Aquinas."[2]

Schleiermacher's apologetic took a different form. Faced by the scepticism of the cultured world, he withdrew religion from the fields of knowing and doing (science and morality) into that of feeling. He postulated a complete discontinuity between the first two spheres and the third. But the result of this withdrawal will be that science and morality will lay

[1] *Op. cit.*, I, p. 21.   [2] *Ibid.*, p. 22.

B

claim to deal with all the realities, and that in the end religion
will be left with no data. Schleiermacher locates the basis of
religion in pure subjectivity.

The argument proceeds as follows: "The men whom we
must now go on to study are all Protestants and all Germans
[*sic*], who (for all their differences among themselves and from
Schleiermacher) have 'tended to accept the fact that religion
must resign all claims on science and morality; that there is
no continuity between the exercise of reason in these spheres
and the awareness of God, and that therefore the data which
prevents [*sic*] the end of theism is to be found through or in
the existential awareness of faith alone'. (This 'faith alone', as
we shall see, is no theological accident. Was not *sola fide* on
the banner of the Reformation?"[1]

That is, for David Jenkins the collapse of men's understanding of transcendence today is due to the sharp split between
reason and revelation made by these Protestant theologians
and implicit in the Reformation. The solution to the difficulty
today is therefore to be found in a repristination of natural
theology, such a natural theology as is to be found in the
Analogy of Joseph Butler.

A similar view is expressed by Professor Eric Mascall. In
a sentence or two, this is that the loss of the sense of transcendence in modern theology is a direct result of, and reaction
from, the extreme doctrine of transcendence of Karl Barth,
Emil Brunner and other modern Protestant theologians. If
the gap between faith and human reason be made so wide and
deep as these thinkers have made it, if all natural knowledge
of God be denied, will not the inevitable reaction follow, that
the trenscendent God will be banished to the sphere of the
irrational? Instead of thus being exalted, will his name not
then soon be declared a sound without meaning, as van
Buren now claims it is? In fact, van Buren himself provides a
very pretty example of this swing-over, since he was a student
under Barth, and we can see the transition in progress in his
own book *The Secular Meaning of the Gospel.*

[1] *Op. cit.*, p. 50.

It is worth documenting this case from Professor Mascall's own writings, for he puts it with considerable force and persuasiveness. Mascall quotes what he calls a remarkably frank passage from van Buren's book as follows: "We reject the cognitive approach to theological language, however, not primarily because it is logically puzzling, but because of certain theological commitments out of which this study has arisen. That approach builds its case on a natural sense of the divine, on natural religion and a natural revelation. The history of theology, seen from the perspective of modern kerygmatic theology, suggests that this is a road leading into the wilderness. Within the Protestant tradition, that road has been clearly charted and firmly marked with a 'dead-end' sign by the work of Karl Barth, and we see no reason to ignore the warning."[1] Mascall's claim here is that van Buren's denial of the transcendence of God, and his assertion of the meaninglessness of the very concept of God is the logical implication of Barth's veto on natural revelation and natural theology.

Mascall claims further that the same baleful influences lie behind the inadequate views of John Robinson on divine transcendence. Speaking on page 119 of his book on the influence of Tillich, Bonhoeffer and Bultmann on Robinson, he says, "Their importance in the present context is through their function as providing the seminal principles for Robinson's own thought. It is, however, interesting that they all come from the background of German Protestantism, and that they all, in different ways, represent the reaction within German Protestantism from the extreme revelationism and supernaturalism of the school of Barth, Brunner and Heim. It has indeed been suggested that the emphatic secularist note which characterised Tillich, Bonhoeffer and Bultmann, to say nothing of Robinson himself, is the product of a violent swing from one extreme to the other, from a position which is all about God and grace to one which is all about man and nature. It is interesting to speculate what kind of book

[1] Van Buren, *The Secular Meaning of the Gospel*, p. 98 (quoted by Mascall in *The Secularisation of Christianity*, p. 63).

Robinson might have written if he had had behind him the
Catholic tradition, with its doctrine of grace as perfecting
nature and not as destroying it."

Finally, Dr. Mascall refers us to an article by Mr. Don
Cupitt in *Theology*[1] which the latter was provoked to write by
reading van Buren. Cupitt, says Mascall, has raised bluntly
the question whether the Gospel is about God or about Jesus.
Most people will say it is about both. Traditional theology
with its insistence that the Gospel is about God implies that
we have some knowledge about God before the Gospel. The
Gospel states that it is the holy God in whom we already
believed, whom ignorantly we worshipped, whose true nature
is now finally declared in Jesus. If someone holds that we have
no knowledge about God apart from Jesus, and also holds
that Jesus is like God, then nothing can tell either for or
against this alleged revelation except the authority of the
revealer. And Mascall concludes thus: "Cupitt's own position
is firmly on the side of the traditional theology, with its
conviction that we can have some knowledge of God prior to
the Gospel; this he maintains was the position not only of the
apologists, but also (whatever the 'neo-orthodox' may say)
of St. Paul. The Gospel, in short, *must* presuppose a natural
theology." "Here, I believe," Mascall concludes, "he is
entirely right. It is, however, ironical that the extreme revelationism of the Barthians, for whom God was everything and
man nothing, should have led to the Christian atheism for
which the man Jesus is everything, and God nothing, in spite
of the difficulty which Cupitt remarks, that Jesus both believed
in, and prayed to God his Father."[2]

My own sympathies are wholly on Cupitt's side as against
van Buren; but there are several holes in the argument, of
which I shall provisionally content myself with mentioning
only two. *First*, the Bible itself never commits us to a valid
natural theology, but rather to a general revelation which
does provide a certain knowledge about God outside of

[1] (LVIII, 1964, pp. 343 ff.)
[2] *Secularisation of Christianity*, pp. 104-5.

Christ.[1] Paul's words, "Whom therefore ye ignorantly worship", bear witness both to the general revelation, and to the distortion in man's response to it. And *secondly*, if Cupitt's and Mascall's argument were right, then conversions from atheism would be impossible. Yet such have been known![2]

And now we come to state the case as posed by the advocates on the other side. The thesis of the Barthians, you will remember, is that the wasting disease of modern faith is due not to too little natural theology but to too much. Any elements of natural theology admitted will tend, they claim, to distort and pervert our understanding, in proportion as they predominate, and will make us incapable of hearing and appropriating God's transcendent revelation.

This is the lesson which underlies a book like Kenneth Hamilton's *Revolt against Heaven*, which gives its own interpretation of the theological history of the last two hundred years, one very different from that of David Jenkins. Just as Jenkins does not stand alone, so neither does Hamilton. This interpretation underlies Barth's work, he has been its greatest twentieth-century exponent. One of its most striking earlier expositions was given in Emil Brunner's *Mediator*, and it is expounded very forcibly by H. J. Iwand in his book *Glauben und Wissen*.

Hamilton's main thesis in his books is as follows. Schleiermacher was the main exponent of a theology which has held the front of the stage for well over a century. The theology of the Word, whose greatest exponent was Karl Barth, was a revolt from this and a return to the faith of the Reformers. At the moment, however, a Schleiermacherian type of theology is attempting a come-back. Its main positive characteristic has been its assertion, in one form or another, openly, or by implication, of an unbroken continuity between God and man. There are a great many variants on this theme, but all of them are in principle opposed to supernaturalism, which Hamilton would define as the conviction that man does not have this immediate and unbroken continuity with God.

[1] For a fuller exposition of the point see Chapter III.
[2] See Appendix B, p. 110.

Were the relationship innate in man, he would in principle be able to tell himself the good news, and to save himself. A common feature of such theologies is therefore a reduced doctrine of the person and work of Christ. But in reality the gospel is good news which we cannot tell to ourselves, and which we must let God say to us in Christ.

Now the exponents of the great and varied Schleiermacherian school, basing themselves on the illusion of unbroken unity between God and man, draw thence norms by which they judge and interpret the revelation in Christ, and cut it down to fit into their preconceived systems. Thus they claim to present to their contemporaries a theology which the latter may be able to understand and accept. Hamilton calls these theologies which he opposes "theologies of meaningfulness". This term is perhaps unfortunate, since it suggests that a theology opposed to this type is not meaningful. The result of these systematic interpretations is that the true gospel presented in the Bible is not able to gain a hearing. And there is a further misfortune. The theologies of meaningfulness are indeed in ultimate principle one, but they present also among themselves a great and contradictory variety. Each theologian has his own form, slanted to what he believes the particular outlook of his day to be. So that the very variety of views offered of the doctrine of God and the Person and Work of Christ is puzzling, and in the end frustrating. Here I might quote a couple of sentences of Iwand which describe the situation. "The godlessness, which we see rampant in the modern world is nothing but the result of the realisation that man is the creator of his gods, his conceptions of God."[1] Again, "This is the godlessness of the modern world. It is not the idolatry of the heathen, but it is the despair and fury of the man who has deceived himself by means of his idea of God, and has led himself by the nose."[2]

From this point Hamilton and the theologians of the Word go on to ask, "What are these different theological systems based on the supposed unbroken continuity between God and

[1] *Glauben und Wissen*, p. 158.   [2] *Ibid.*, p. 164.

man, but various types of natural theology?" We will not confuse them with the old Thomist-type of natural theology, which was a comparatively harmless affair. It claimed on rational grounds to establish certain elementary conclusions about God. Beyond, there was a whole realm of revealed Christian doctrine which could only be accepted on the authority of Scripture and the Church. This type of thinking Schleiermacher repudiated. But his own type of natural theology was built up on the belief in a fundamental unity between God and man. This unity was reflected subjectively in the feeling of absolute dependence. And the assumption of this unity controlled in Schleiermacher's theology the whole interpretation of the Christian faith. It did so in a way that the Thomistic natural theology was never allowed to control the Thomistic theological system, where natural theology had to give way to revealed theology in all the higher matters of doctrine. What is true of Schleiermacher is true also of other theologies of the same type.

The exponents of the Theology of the Word further make great play, and with some justification, of the continually changing interpretations of God and Christ offered by the various theologies of meaningfulness. Shakespeare once wrote:

> Imperious Caesar, dead and turned to clay,
> Might stop a hole to keep the wind away.

Might it not be said that the theologians who claim to fit God and Christ into their continually changing and transitory systems as the coping-stone have, in all good faith, been guilty of a cosmic act of vandalism far greater than the human vandalism of which Hamlet spoke? Their intention was to honour the God whom they knew in faith; for a man's faith, as Karl Barth often reminds us, is often far better than his theology. But the result, in the end, was confusion.

Here then, with the statement of these contradictory diagnoses and prescriptions, we come to the end of the first chapter. We started by recognising the recent tremors in the world of faith and theology. Clearly an attack was being made on the concept of divine transcendence, Many of our contemporaries were intolerant of this notion. So the concept of transcendence was obviously one that required, as it was already receiving, attention in theological thinking. And then in closing we looked at the fresh interest which theologians have found in reconsidering and interpreting the history of thought which has led to the difficulties of today.

We have considered two apparently contradictory interpretations of the past and its significance for the Church and theological work today. At the moment there appears to be great difficulty in avoiding a choice between them, but it may become clear that there are truths behind both viewpoints, and that something is to be learnt from both.

One further thing must be said. It will be asked, and with apparent justice, whether the whole approach of this chapter has not been a symptom of the ghetto mentality of the Church and theology today. It may be asked whether the assumption underlying what is said here is not that modern man has lost the sense of transcendence because theologians have admitted too much, or too little, natural theology into their studies, and preachers into their sermons, and whether this is not a preposterous bit of conceit? Are there not vast influences at work of a quite different kind which have caused the present climate of thought in the world? For example, the prestige of science and technology, which tempts men to think that scientific thought is the paradigm of all knowing and that statements which cannot stand up to a scientific kind of verification are illusion or nonsense?

Of course this is true, and in a full-length study this would have to be stated as it deserves. But the question of the theologian's ultimate loyalties is really of first-rate importance, and it is this issue which is here at stake. Our task is the understanding of the Christian faith and its presentation to the world. In order to know what the gospel is in the world of today, and in order to distinguish it from false gospels, theologians must have a right understanding of God's transcendence. And that is the theme of our present study.

CHAPTER II

The Interpretation of Transcendence

THE Oxford Dictionary gives the following definition of the word *transcendence*: "Of the Deity, the attribute of being above and independent of the universe, distinguished from immanence". This definition will do for a start. We must note that these two terms, "transcendent" and "immanent" and two other terms often used in the same context—"supernatural" and "natural"—are not to be found anywhere in the Bible, though of course many passages could be quoted as illustrating what these words mean.

The concept of the transcendence of God is in danger of becoming as much of a wax nose which anyone can pull in any direction, or mould between warm finger and thumb, as is the concept of the supernatural—at present so much in disgrace among fashionable theologians. Roman Catholic theology means one thing by it, Oman meant another, Farmer another, Tillich christened it in Teutonic fashion the supranatural—in my opinion his conception of it is a mere caricature. Kenneth Hamilton has yet another definition.

In order if possible to avoid the same kind of confusion in relation to our chosen theme, I shall do my best to speak of that transcendence of God which is central to the biblical revelation. All my attempts to define and to distinguish, to argue and occasionally to refute, will be made with an eye kept continually on that revelation as the source and norm, thinking out the implications for our own thought today. This will be no easy task, but at any rate it is the aim of this study.

Included in the notion of transcendence is of course the idea of reality, of objectivity in the wide sense of the word. Part of the debate in theology is carried on in confrontation with types of thinking which deliberately deny the reality of

God. Freud, Feuerbach and Durkheim are all exponents of systems which deny his reality. Most of our discussion, however, will deal with thinkers who are in danger of involuntarily denying and dissolving that reality, and dissolving it, for example, in a fog of self-understanding.

But the transcendence of God raises other problems than those raised by the reality, the transcendence of, say, other human beings. For God is not a public object, he is transcendent *par excellence* and what his transcendence means can be seen best by an examination of the biblical witness to it.

After this introduction it will be most to our purpose if I try to indicate what is the doctrine of God contained in the biblical revelation, so that we may have the biblical account of transcendence, obviously only in the merest outline, before us. Here I shall set forth in brief form the teaching of Emil Brunner, as expounded in the first volume of his *Dogmatics*. Brunner is a good example of a modern theologian who is determined to be true to this account, seeking at each point to show where metaphysics or natural theology has distorted and misled Christian teaching. It is true that Bishop Nygren[1] thinks that Brunner has not been entirely successful in this task, but has to some extent himself fallen a victim to a personalist philosophy—but we shall leave this criticism on one side and take Brunner's as an admirable exposition within reasonable length of the biblical doctrine of God's transcendence.

Brunner, in my opinion rightly, rejects an eclectic approach which gathers together from different parts of the Bible a number of quotations, grouping them according to themes. His attempt to set forth the biblical doctrine takes hold of a number of central concepts. Here I must give a warning. The Bible is not interested in the cool and dispassionate study of a theme like God's transcendence. Its aim all through is the proclamation of a central message which is addressed to man's heart and conscience. It is only when theological thought has been disturbed by questionings and new projects of thought

[1] Cr. *The Theology of Emil Brunner*, pp. 178-86.

have been put forward claiming to replace old conceptions
that it becomes necessary to raise such a question as this—
"What *is*, after all, the biblical conception of God's transcendence?"

The Bible, says Brunner, teaches that God is a mystery
withdrawn from us; by searching we cannot find him out.
Only if he reveals himself can he be known. What he reveals
is his name. This is the first great biblical concept to which
Brunner draws our attention. The name of Jahweh was at
first used to distinguish him from other gods. These gods were
later shown to be nothingness, yet the name of God continues
to be central. In his prayer to the Father, Jesus said of his
disciples, "I have revealed unto them thy name". Why has
the name of God this incomparable place in the Bible?
Because God is over against us, the living God, who calls us
into fellowship and covenant with him. His name is the unity
of his revealing action and his revealed nature. By imparting
to men his name he gives them a right to call upon him.

The second concept Brunner selects is that of lordship
(*Herrsein*); God reveals himself as the Lord. As the Lord he
was from the first distinguished from the nature-gods, who
also received a name indicating lordship—Baal. But God is
known, not as a power of nature, but through his mighty acts
in history. Later it becomes explicit that he is Lord over
nature also.

Thirdly, God is the Holy One. As the Holy One of Israel
he is distinguished from all else. He is different from the
created world. Hence the veto on idols. This holiness means
that he is not indifferent to man's response but infinitely
concerned. There are two movements in his holiness. God
alone is holy; this is the movement of exclusiveness. But his
holiness has in it also a moment of inclusion, of movement
towards men. He desires them to be holy, and in a secondary
sense his people also is holy.

Lastly, God is love. This is a love which has no need of the
loved object, but in outflowing, ungrounded generosity desires
to create, and then to give itself to the creature, so that he

may share in the supreme gift of holiness and life of fellowship
with God. There is no contradiction between God's love and
his holiness. God's holiness shows itself as wrath in the face of
rejection, but this is only the reverse side of his infinite and
consuming love. God's lordship manifests itself supremely in
his forgiveness of sinners, and here he shows himself free from,
and above, his own laws—and able by this self-sacrificing love
to win man over to repentance and responding love. And all
this without infringing man's freedom. Here is the supreme
revelation of God's power and his transcendence.

Brunner now makes a distinction of importance and some
difficulty, which must here be taken into account. These
realities of which we have been speaking, God's Name, his
lordship (*Herrsein*) his holiness, his love, belong to his nature.
That which belongs to his nature is his, apart from his relation
to the created world. Brunner then distinguishes God's nature
from his attributes. The attributes flow from his nature, and
express it in his relation to his creation.

Three remarks have to be made at this point.

First, we sometimes hear it said that we cannot know God
as he is in himself, but only as he is in his relation to us.
Sometimes an even greater subjectivism is lurking near, when
it is said or implied that we cannot know God, but only his
effects upon us, on our self-understanding in the encounter
with him. Brunner's distinction between God's nature and his
attributes is not tainted with this subjectivism. Brunner affirms
that both in his nature and his attributes God himself is really
known to faith.

The second point is a real difficulty, but it need not detain
us very long. We may ask whether God's lordship (*Herrsein*)
is conceivable without a created universe of which he is Lord.
Brunner says "Yes". In himself he is Lord, and the created
universe is the expression of the free creative love which is
God's. He did not *have* to create a world: it is not an inevitable
emanation from his being. It owes its existence to his free
decision to give his infinite riches to a created universe.

Third, a similar difficulty arises in regard to God's love.

Can there be love without a created other to love? Brunner sometimes answers this problem in the same way; this free love of God created a universe and finite spirits who could benefit by it. In himself God is this love, which does not need a universe, though it created one. Sometimes Brunner deals with this difficulty by referring to that difference within God's trinitarian nature which means that there was always a Son and a Father to love him. I think that only if *this* is the case can we define God in his nature as love. Otherwise, apart from the created world he would only be love potentially.

With regard to God's *attributes*, which express his nature in relation to his created world—we may list among these God's power over the created world, his *Allmacht*. The word "Omnipotence" (*omnipotentia*) is disliked by Brunner because it has been so loaded with false speculative content. This is, the word "Omnipotence" very easily gives rise to such a conception of God's absolute power as drains all reality from his creation, and pantheism results. This is worlds away from the biblical conception of God's power, a power which always takes thought for the reality of his creatures and their limited freedom. For this conception Brunner uses the word *Allmacht*. God's *Allmacht* is that attribute of God in relation to the created world which arises from the Lordship (*Herrsein*) of his nature. Similarly, God's eternity is not a mark of his *nature*, but an attribute of his in relation to time, which is a created magnitude. So that we are not to think of creation as an event in time, for time itself is a created magnitude. And God's eternity is not to be regarded, as Platonism held, as timeless, for this again will empty the life-blood out of time and history. We can only conceive of God's eternity as expressing his lordship over time. His omnipresence and his eternity mean that there is no place and no time in which he is not at hand to govern and to help, to guide and to overrule. Thus Brunner keeps true to the given historical revelation and does not attempt to conceive of eternity in a speculative way.

Such is Brunner's attempt to give a picture of the biblical conception of God's transcendence, and I could have given a very similar picture from Barth, or one of the other "theologians of the Word", as Kraemer calls them. The question which we must now answer is this: Do we not have here, taking it all in all, a fair, powerful and faithful exposition of the biblical notion of transcendence? I might even go further and say that any exposition of transcendence which in matters of first importance departs from this is not true to the biblical outlook.

We must next consider an objection which is often made nowadays to what Tillich calls "supranaturalism", and to what Gregor Smith and others call the metaphysical notion of transcendence. In general, this objection is formulated thus: that this supranaturalism divides reality sharply into two spheres, a natural sphere and a supernatural one, all emphasis in the end being laid upon the latter, and all reality drained from history, in which men have to live, so that a chilling and hopeless dualism is the eventual outcome.

Tillich describes supranaturalism as "a way of interpreting the meaning of the term 'God' as one that separates God as a being, the highest being, from all other beings, alongside and above which he has his existence. In this position he has brought the universe into being at a certain moment (five thousand or five billion years ago), governs it according to a plan, directs it towards an end, interferes with its ordinary processes in order to overcome resistance and to fulfil his purposes, and will bring it to consummation in a final catastrophe. Certainly this is a primitive form of supranaturalism, but a form which is more decisive for the religious life and its symbolic expression than any theological refinement of this position."[1]

Tillich gives his objections to this view: "The main argument against it is that it transforms the infinity of God into a finiteness which is merely an extension of the categories of finitude. This is done in respect to space by establishing a supranatural divine world alongside the natural human world, in respect to time by determining a beginning and an end of God's creativity, in respect to cause by making God a cause

[1] *Systematic Theology*, Vol. I, p. 6.

alongside the natural human world, in respect to substance by attributing individual substance to him."[1]

Now it appears that without a certain dualism no justice can be done to the biblical conception of transcendence. As Gregor Smith has written. "It is the truth, so simple and yet so hard, that God is not the world. Nor is he man. Between God and the world, and between God and man, there is a infinite qualitative difference. God is wholly different from man. Between God and man there is a gulf which man cannot bridge."[2] In his revelation God has both revealed and crossed this gulf, but it remains. And any interpretation of God's transcendence which is true to the Bible must do justice to this fundamental reality. We shall have occasion in the last chapter of this book to revert to the implications of the biblical conception of God's transcendence. But the question which must now be put is this: Does such an exposition of God's transcendence as Brunner has given fall under the condemnation of dividing the natural world from the supernatural, and time from eternity, in such a way that time, history and human freedom are drained of all reality and significance?

My own answer would be that Brunner comes out triumphantly from this challenge, just because of his essential faithfulness to the biblical doctrine of transcendence and his rejection of speculative and natural theology. All the time he remains, as it were, in the sub-lunar world he does not try to stand outside of it. He expounds what God is for faith. God's own nature is indeed known to faith. Brunner avers that apart from his creation he is the holy Lord, he is love, and is known as such, but surely this is an essential content of the revelation and not a piece of speculation. In his teaching about God's attributes, Brunner refuses to describe God's almighty power (his *Allmacht*) and his eternity as part of his nature. Philosophical speculation in theology, by doing so, has given such a definition of God's omnipotence as drains off all reality from the created world, and all freedom from created wills. And again, by its definition of God's eternity as timelessness,

---

[1] *Ibid.*　　　　[2] *Secular Christianity*, p. 21.

speculation has also drained off all reality from history and time.

Brunner insists that we remain by that definition of the power of God (*Allmacht*) which is necessary for faith—it is an attribute of God in relation to history; God has power over history. Thus God's eternity is defined as his power over created time, a power which respects the reality of the creation which he has made. It seems to me that this interpretation is an implicate of faith, and that this doctrine, by its restraint from the speculations of natural theology, is true to the biblical revelation, and at the same time avoids the evil consequences denounced by writers like Tillich and Smith.

I wish next to make clear my position in relation to two contemporary writers, Kenneth Hamilton and Edward Farley. Kenneth Hamilton (to be carefully distinguished from his namesake William) has made a distinction between biblical and metaphysical transcendence. In his able book *Revolt against Heaven* he writes: "If transcendence be taken in its simplest and most straightforward sense of 'the quality of going beyond or being superior to', it will be seen to apply to any idea of God whatsoever. In the most primitive faiths the gods are more powerful than man. And where one God alone is worshipped, this God has no competitor in heaven either, for he has outpaced all other deities until these have simply dropped out of sight."[1] It is clear from Hamilton's supporting citations of Isaiah and Ezekiel that here he has Hebrew monotheism in view, adding that in it, "through concrete realistic words, the imagination gives form to the experience of a revelation of religious transcendence".

In the second place, Hamilton says, "However, transcendence may be a term employed in the realm of conceptual thinking as well as in the realm of worship and living faith. In this case the simple meaning is transformed in the service of logic to become that which can be predicated of a philosophical absolute", and he goes on to say that here the transcendent is directly linked with a world-view, "it is the coping-

[1] P. 49.

stone of a particular metaphysical system; the philosophers' God is the transcendent within a specified cosmology".[1] And Hamilton goes on to describe how, as one metaphysical system or world-view supplants another, one conception of the transcendent will supplant another until the student of metaphysical systems grows dizzy.[2]

We are thus left with the feeling that instead of God being the creator of the metaphysician, the metaphysician has become the creator of God—his own god, whose fate it will be to collapse with the inevitable collapse of the metaphysician's system. There is a truth here, and the simple believer cannot help exclaiming, when confronted with various theological or metaphysical systems, each one different and each one more imposing than the last, that "they can't *all* be right". Yet each one of them proclaims itself so confidently to be "the mostest" and "the bestest". In view of this rivalry, there is help in the reflection that all of them, even the most impressive, are merely the utterances of mortal clay. This comfort we may take to ourselves from Hamilton's argument, though we may feel that what he says here is in some ways unfortunate and misleading. My reasons for this are two.

Firstly, as he himself indicates, were there not the *experience*[3] of the transcendent, the philosophers would never have tried to construct the concept and give it a place in their systems. That we judge these interpretations of the philosophers to have gone astray is another matter. If they do go astray, and lead to false interpretations of transcendence, they are to be repudiated.

Secondly, the Christian's experience of transcendence in revelation is never pure experience without the texture of thought in it. For example, a simple believer may be able to repudiate wrong interpretations of God's transcendence, even though he may not be able to give a clear reason for doing so. But this repudiation shows that there is already interpretation and intellectual understanding in his faith. It is, accordingly,

---

[1] *Revolt against Heaven*, p. 50. [2] *Ibid.*, pp. 50-2.
[3] I use the word "experience" in its widest sense.

C

the Christian theologian's duty to try to formulate what is
implied in the Christian experience of God's transcendence.
And this is not wicked, but a task laid upon him by his faith.
If the theologian errs, then the project is not to be abandoned
but a new start is to be made. Kenneth Hamilton's contrast
could too easily be misunderstood as an attempt to throw the
experience of revelation into a sheer opposition with intellectual reflection upon it. And this could lead to a breakdown
of theological thought and dialogue with the world, and
Christianity's retreat into a biblicist ghetto. That this is not
Hamilton's intention is evident from the last chapter of
his book on Tillich, *The System and the Gospel*, where he urges
the necessity of just such a dialogue. Here I wish to quote with
full approval a statement of Gollwitzer's. "At all events a
theological ontology cannot . . . make a peace of partition
with noncompatible elements of a philosophical ontology,
but must take issue with them, since it does not mean a reality
other than what is the reality of us all, and is therefore not a
ghetto science, but must stake a claim to truth that is universal,
i.e., valid for all."[1] I would here suggest, and I am sure that
Hamilton would agree, that it is not our thinking conceptually
about transcendence that is the mistake, but the placing of
our final loyalty in the wrong place. Is our thinking to be
guided by biblical revelation, or by a system of natural
theology? Here our discipline is to be one of apologetic or
eristic and not that of natural theology.

I would at this point suggest that here we may have the
answer to a problem that faced us at the end of the first chapter.
Confronted by the contemporary predicament about the
transcendence of God, one school of theologians says that it
is due to too much natural theology, and another school that
it is due to too little natural theology. Might it not be that,
strictly speaking, the first school are right? Natural theologians
of different schools have offered so many different interpretations of transcendence that the result has been confusion and
satiety. Further, natural theology always distorts and mis-

---

[1] *The Existence of God as Confessed by Faith*, p. 213.

represents the revelational truth which it seeks to interpret. But there is a truth in what the advocates of natural theology maintain, that members of the school of biblical theology have often been unwilling to advance into the world of modern thought and discussion, and to expound in contemporary terms how the biblical conception of transcendence and other kindred concepts are to be expressed for the men of today, in the very different climate of thought in which we of the twentieth century have to live. It is possible to repeat "The Bible teaches" in such a way that thought is dulled rather than stimulated, and a real encounter of Christian conviction with contemporary ways of thought is avoided rather than encouraged. So to state biblical thought in its relation to the modern situation is, however, not the task of natural theology, but of *apologetic*, or as Emil Brunner alternatively, though perhaps hardly more happily, described it, eristic theology. The present study is conceived as a modest contribution in this field.

Here a reference must be made to Edward Farley's book *The Transcendence of God*[1]. In his first chapter Farley makes a contrast between what he calls kerygmatic and metaphysical transcendence. Here he seems to be making nearly the same distinction as Hamilton makes with his terms "The Biblical and Metaphysical Interpretations of Transcendence". Certainly Farley's kerygmatic transcendence covers the same ground as Hamilton's "Biblical Interpretations of Transcendence." Farley writes, "The kerygma technically is that central message of good news preached by apostles and evangelists in New Testament times. . . . Such transcendence is thus not so much known as confessed, for it is derived from a faithful response to the Word."[2]

It is rather hard to discover what Farley means by "metaphysical transcendence", for at this point his writing is imprecise. Perhaps his meaning appears from the following paragraph. "It is the thesis of this study that contemporary theology has come to more or less of an *impasse* between

[1] See also Appendix A, p. 106. [2] P. 37.

kerygmatic and metaphysical types of theology. Assuming that
God is both the transcendent one who is given in the Word
made flesh, and the metaphysical *ens realissimum*, what is the
relation between the two? How are we to relate, to use Pascal's
words "the God of the philosophers, and the God of Abraham,
Isaac and Jacob?".[1] It would appear from this statement that
for Farley metaphysical transcendence is the transcendence
reached as an ultimate principle by a philosophy which
defines God as the absolute or most real being.

Now I would be most unwilling to commit myself to a type
of philosophy which regards God as pure being, with its
accompanying doctrine of the analogy of being regarded as
an independent source of our knowledge of God. But we
cannot affirm a theology which believes, or claims to believe,
in the God of Abraham and then fails to affirm that as such
he is the final reality. Such a theology would be a contradiction
in terms. The question we must put to the creators of metaphysical systems is this, "Do you believe that as philosophers you
have such access to the knowledge of being as will enable you
to judge, and, it may be, to relativise the claims made on
behalf of the God of Abraham, Isaac and Jacob? Where do
you place your final loyalty? With the God of revelation, or
your independent knowledge of being?"

Farley has confused the issues here by suggesting that the
exponents of kerygmatic transcendence are interested in
epistemological problems and not in ontological problems.[2]
That is, they are interested in the question "How do we know
God?" but not in the question "What is God's relation to his
world?" This is surely a quite impossible antithesis between
knowing and reality which kerygmatic theologians would one
and all repudiate. The God of Abraham cannot be known
without being at the same time acknowledged as the supreme
reality, the creator of, and different from, the created universe.

[1] P. 41.
[2] *Op. cit.*, p. 38. But on p. 204 he expresses himself much more moderately,
and discusses not only how God's transcendence is known, but also what
its nature is.

My general conclusion is that Farley has unfortunately left without a clear answer this most important question of our ultimate loyalty, which is surely the one central, vital question at this point.[1]

It is, however, only fair to repeat that once we know where our ultimate loyalty lies, we are not able simply to override all discussion by saying without further thought, "The Bible teaches", "Christians believe". We are given into our hands no principle which will enable us to approach any theological work, for example, the ontological theology of Paul Tillich, or the personalist theology of Emil Brunner, and decide off the cuff what is true and what is false. We are left with the often intensely difficult task of considering every theology that claims to be a faithful interpretation of the biblical faith, and reflecting long and carefully as to whether this theology is what it claims to be. In that inquiry we must be guided by our assessment of what is merely timebound in the biblical records, and what is central and essential to the life of the Christian faith.

[1] See also Appendix A, p. 106.

CHAPTER III

Is There a Generally Revealed Transcendence of God?

FROM the title of this chapter the reader will see that once more the old question of general revelation is being raised. I am, however, raising it only in so far as it bears upon our special theme, and even within these limits our discussion will be summary. Almost a generation ago there was a bitter debate on this subject, which left behind it a certain exhaustion, confusion of mind and even disgust.

The air has, however, to some extent cleared since then, and in a discussion dealing with God's transcendence we cannot leave unasked the question as to whether that transcendence is or can be, revealed outwith the revelation to which the Bible bears sole and central witness. I say "sole and central witness" for there can be no question of the fact that in addition to its witness to God as the God of Abraham, Isaac and Jacob, the God and Father of Jesus Christ, the Bible bears witness also to what we may call his general revelation, or, as Emil Brunner has put it, his revelation in creation. Of course the God revealed is the one God, and there is no contradiction between the two revelations, as the Bible understands them. God is supremely the God of Jesus Christ, and in the light of Christ's revelation all other revelations must be judged, but the Bible bears undiscordant testimony to the fact that there is no race among men where God has not borne some witness to himself.

The terms in which this general revelation was affirmed by Emil Brunner, and violently denied by Karl Barth and his followers, need not be discussed yet once more in detail. The virulence of the anathemas pronounced against Brunner is perhaps explicable, though hardly excusable, because they arose from a misunderstanding, the misunderstanding that here a door was being reopened to the pagan Nazi doctrine of revelation through blood and soil, a door which the Barmen Declaration of the Confessing Church had bravely slammed shut in 1933.

Since then tempers have cooled and reassessments have been made. One of the most powerful and important studies in this field was written by Hendrik Kraemer in 1956—in his second great book, *Religion and the Christian Faith*, which develops, clarifies and in certain ways corrects his earlier work, *The Christian Message in a non-Christian World*, written for the Tambaram Conference in 1938. I am in almost entire agreement with this second book, which incidentally to its central theme takes on the whole the part of Brunner against Barth while drawing attention to the dangers present in the ambiguity of the terms "general and special revelation". These terms, Kraemer tells us, are too convenient as a means for delineating two very important realities for it to be probable that they will be soon dropped, if ever.[1] But because of the past history of the Church it is only too easy for us to think of general revelation as consisting of a number of doctrines whose truth is sometimes regarded as demonstable by reason, while special revelation consists of a number of further doctrines not accessible to reason but guaranteed by authority or miracle. But to think thus is to have moved far away from the biblical conception of the living God who never forgets his human creatures but is always approaching all of them in grace. If, therefore, we are to use these terms, general and special revelation, we must guard against this intellectualism which has been too much associated with their use and bend them back into obedience to the truth.

One of Kraemer's central theses is that God has revealed and continues to reveal to all men his love and his righteous wrath. This wrath is simply the obverse of his love, its intolerance of evil. From this evil he seeks to deliver men. In response to this revelation in creation there is among men, inextricably

[1] *Religion and the Christian Faith*, chapter XX, "General and Special Revelation".

intermingled, the twofold response of a search for and longing for God, and of a flight from him and revolt against him. God maintains thus a living dialogue with men to which the Bible bears continual witness. Nowhere does the Bible seek a direct point of contact with the religions of the Gentiles, in the sense of regarding itself as affirming them or fulfilling them. It rather bears witness to God's original revelation to which other religions are in part a positive and in part a negative, hostile response. In view of this conclusion, supported by prolonged, fair and penetrating biblical exegeses, Kraemer rejects the suggestion that the religions could serve as a *praeperatio evangelica* for the revelation in Christ, in the sense that it could be regarded simply as their fulfilment and crown. The same is true of the relation of the special revelation to man's wisdom and culture. While these are seen as not without God, and indeed even as gifts of God, there is shown to be a reversal of human wisdom in the purpose of God and the Cross. The need for this reversal is due to man's perversion of God's gifts, which he uses to secure an unlawful independence for himself. This is the judgement of the independent "theologian of the Word", Hendrik Kraemer, who describes himself also as a biblical realist.

Today it seems that also among the theologians who stand somewhat closer to Karl Barth there is also a re-assessment of the unfavourable verdict passed in the thirties and forties upon Emil Brunner. A very fair and able book on Brunner's doctrine of man[1] was presented for a doctorate in 1965 by Roman Roessler under Helmut Gollwitzer's tutelage and guidance. This book may go far to securing among the Barthians a posthumous free pardon for Brunner for a crime which he did not commit.

The time has come now to point out the fuller significance of a statement made in the last chapter. There it was said that if there had not been among men the experience of transcendence, no philosopher would have tried to make the idea of the transcendent the coping-stone of his philosophy. I believe

[1] *Person und Glaube.*

that such attempts are vain, but that is another matter. What is to the point now is the fact that man's experience of the transcendent is not confined to the historical revelation, the special and central revelation of the Christian faith. The transcendent is presented to man also in God's continual dialogue with him through the general revelation. In my examination of the meaning of transcendence I shall try to take into account what it may mean in this realm also. And it must be repeated that what is being said here is spoken from the standpoint of a Christian believer. We are not just analysing the concept of transcendence in general, but endeavouring to grasp the content of that word enriched and determined by the whole Christian and biblical understanding of God and his relation to the world. Yet it is God's transcendence in general revelation seen by the Christian which is our theme in this chapter.

I wish next to point out that when the word "general" is employed by me in this context, the word indicates that this is a revelation directed continually by God to all his human creatures, a dialogue in which, as Kraemer says, God never lets go his hold of his children. If we use the word "general", we do not thereby mean "public". If this revelation were public, in the sense that no reasonable man could deny it, or if it were general in such a way that man, by a study of his own nature, or of the moral law within or the starry heavens without, could by a chain of reasoning prove that God exists, then surely such a revelation would not be revelation in any true sense at all. God would be caught in the web of our reasoning, disclosed without mystery. He would indeed be a part of the world and not transcendent in any radical sense at all. This reflection is surely enough to make us realise that when we are conversing about these matters together, or with the atheist or doubter, we are reasoning in a singular manner. This is a field of discourse where nothing like demonstration is to be looked for, but where insights either do, or do not, dawn upon the inquiring mind. Here I would agree with the words of Professor John Baillie: "Thus for the New Testament as for the Old, God is One who is directly known in his approach to the human soul. He is not an inference, but a Presence."[1]

May I interject at this point the comment that I hope the reader will see what I am endeavouring to do. Following Kraemer's advice, I am trying to define general revelation in an existential rather than in a rationalist intellectualist way, as a continuing encounter, not an inference. For this is the way in which I am sure that the Bible regards it. Thus, considered as an approach of the living God to men, calling for a response of gratitude and obedience, it is brought back into kinship with God's central call to men through the historic revelation in Christ.[2]

To sum up what we have been saying—While we may reason with the agnostic about the general, as about the special revelation, in the end it is a matter of seeing or not seeing. We may say that spiritual things are spiritually discerned, provided that we avoid the implication that the man who does not see is necessarily morally inferior to us. There is, of course, as all would agree, such a thing as blindness due to moral defect, but there are people with whom we disagree on these matters whom we must call both morally better and humbler than ourselves. So we have to leave this mystery to God who is its source, and who reveals himself when and where and to whom he will. Any doctrine of revelation and transcendence must refrain from trying to imprison God within his own creation and leave him sovereign freedom to speak to whom, and when and where he will.

Does this mean that we must content ourselves with saying "God can reveal himself anywhere"?—and let that be all we can say about general revelation? I do not think so. Just as we are not restricted to such limits in speaking of special revelation, but are told that God spoke in past times to the fathers by the prophets, and in the latter days through his Son, so it may be legitimate to claim that there are *foci* of the revelation in

---

[1] *Our Knowledge of God*, p. 126.
[2] What is here described is not a continuity between God and man, but a continued gracious approach of God to man.

creation. The man who claims this is surely no more assaulting God's sovereignty than the man who claims that God is finally revealed through Christ.

We have been considering the special nature of this discussion and the special status in reality of the themes it deals with. But if it is a discussion in which no clear-cut logical victory can be hoped for, such as theologians formerly believed was possible, it may be asked, Why is it worth while entering upon the discussion at all? I can think of several cogent reasons for the determination to do so.

First there is the duty laid upon Christians to think through to the best of their ability the Christian doctrines of God and of man. This naturally involves asking what is meant by man's nature and its relationship to God. There are others who will be offering other doctrines of man's nature, mostly expressed in idealist or naturalist terms. We cannot leave the field to them, but must engage with them.

Then, secondly, there is the interpretation of moral responsibility. This is a part of the doctrine of man. Most Christians are agreed in offering some kind of theological interpretation of that responsibility. But it is a central Christian doctrine that all men share in moral responsibility and in guilt, however much variation there may be from man to man. The special revelation does not find man innocent and leave him guilty, it reveals more clearly to him a guilt which he already has. But if we must interpret moral responsibility in theological terms, and if all men are responsible, it follows that there must be a general revelation that constitutes men responsible sinners; all have sinned and come short of the glory of God—that is, the glory of existence in the divine image. This is one of the strongest motives behind Calvin's assertion of a general revelation, and I do not see how his position on this matter can be overturned.

A third reason for entering upon this discussion is the terrible difficulty for faith which would be constituted by the denial of such a revelation. What kind of a Creator and Father-God would he be who had created at such cost, and through such

long ages of history, a race of mankind to whose mind and
conscience he had through all these many thousands of years
succeeded in saying *nothing*, in revealing *nothing* of his own love
and his own purpose? I have heard Karl Barth say, "I love
and admire Socrates, but he knew absolutely nothing of the
true God. There was absolutely nothing in common between
the *daimonion* of Socrates who forbade him to desert the post
of duty, and the true God." If I had to choose between this
position and that of Dr. John Baillie, who wrote in a prayer
the invocation, "God of the first altar, God of the first prayer",
I would choose to side with Baillie, well aware though I am,
as he was, of the demonic perversions to which prayer and
religious sacrifice can fall a victim.

But our main reason for entering upon this discussion must
surely be that we believe the Bible is right in asserting that
there is given such a general revelation, and that accordingly
here is a field of revealed transcendence, of which we dare
not neglect to speak.

I would like to point out yet once more that this discussion,
which is so necessary for the Christian Church, is not natural
theology, for it never seeks to hide the fact that it bases itself
upon the presuppositions of the Christian faith. It does indeed
look at some of the same realities as are the theme of other
disciplines. One of these realities, for example, is the nature of
man. But it does not speak, to use Anselm's phrase, "*Christo
remoto*"—without Christ. This Christian eristic, as Brunner
calls it, is the necessary consequence of the belief that the God
revealed by Christ is the ultimate reality. This eristic is the
necessary working out of what we feel to be the implications
of the faith. Perhaps it is the neglect of this discipline which
some theologians blame for our present theological predicament. And so they go on, inaccurately, to say that neglect of
natural theology is the cause of our troubles, which have
culminated in the "Death of God" theologies.

I now wish to follow up these remarks on the general
revelation by a more detailed discussion of the teaching of
Emil Brunner. My main task will be to consider a question

which arises for the careful student of Brunner's theology. This is the question: "Is there a fundamental contradiction in Brunner's doctrine of general revelation, and consequently in his doctrine of man? Is there a more negative view expressed in those writings of his which deal with the possibility of a natural knowledge of God, as contrasted with a more positive view as implied by his doctrine of man as being essentially a being whose very existence is an answering, responsive existence in and to the Word of God?"

Before I go on to deal with this question, I wish to sketch in the background of Brunner's teaching on the general revelation, condensing what he says in his book *Offenbarung und Vernunft*, which contains the most full and consecutive exposition of his teaching.

Here Brunner tells us that God himself is the subject and the content of the revelation in creation. It is called by this name for two reasons. First, this revelation has been made since the beginning of the world, and secondly, it is given through the works of creation. It can be perceived by an act of reason (*Nous*). Brunner writes: "Thus what is spoken of (in the Bible) is not only a possibility of the knowledge of God which was once present, but now is lost, nor yet a present possibility of knowledge of God, but an actual knowledge, though admittedly a knowledge which in consequence of man's sin is at once transformed into delusion; that is, a knowledge which does not work itself out as knowledge, but is transformed by the ferment of sin into idolatry and delusion".[1]

Thus, according to the Bible, there is no room left for the development, on the basis of general revelation, of a systematic true natural theology which would enable man to know God in spite of his sin, and in it. To put it in different terms, while there is this revelation in creation, and this momentary and continuing knowledge of God, which serves to make man guilty, there is no such thing as a valid natural theology, or system of knowledge built up on the basis of the revelation in creation alone.

[1] *Offenbarung und Vernunft*, p. 64. E.T., p. 64.

At this point Brunner makes the further remark that this general revelation can be seen, and can be rightly interpreted, by the man who is a believer in Christ. He used, so he tells us to call such an understanding a "Christian natural theology", but later—so soon as 1935 in fact—he gave up the use of this name because of its dangerous ambiguity.

While there is no valid natural theology, Brunner continues, natural theologies do in fact exist, claiming to be cogent for reason in general. Brunner avers that these systems inevitably diverge from one another, and that none of them is able to bear down its opponents in argument, as would be the case if the claims of any of the various disputants were justified.

Had we asked Brunner where the revelation in question is to be found, he would, I am sure, have referred us to the created and visible world through which the invisible things of God are manifest; he would, I think further refer us to the moral imperative and, indirectly, to the absolute and normative ideas which give the human spirit its power to think, and its transcendence over the world of process feeling and sensation. Brunner came out of a background of critical idealism, one of his greatest intellectual struggles was an engagement with the thought of Immanuel Kant, and he had to fit in what he learnt from such writers as Natorp and Cohen, in due sub-ordination to what he found in the biblical tradition and the thought of the Reformers. His intellectual need was to do justice to the absolute ideas of the realm of spirit (Geist), and yet in such a way as to avoid the conclusion that by means of these ideas we have such direct access to, or identity with, the Divine Spirit as would provide us with a valid natural theology.

Thus he is always careful to say that we cannot reach the living God along the *Denkweg*—the thought-way. There are in his writings several passages where men's attempts thus to reach God are evaluated, and the limits of what can be attained by them are laid down.

Perhaps his clearest and most satisfactory treatment of this is given in *Offenbarung und Vernunft*, in his chapter on the Logos of Revelation and the Logos of Reason. Here is an abbreviation of a very important passage,[1] "The ideas of goodness, truth and justice are at least in essence the common possession of every man . . . in and through these ideas God works in every man. This belongs to the general revelation which at the same time determines the structure of our humanity. . . . But we do not say that this logos is God's Logos. . . . The idea of the good is the thoroughly abstract and colourless manner in which man, in so far as he is thrown on his own intellectual resources, knows about God the creator and his creative, personal Word. The ideas are only a last weak memory of what we ought to have known of God and his loving personal Word had we been true to our origin."[2] A few pages further on the same kind of thing is said about the moral imperative "In the form of the 'Thou shalt', the Christian man can see a reflection in the spirit of man, as he is, without the Christian revelation, of the fact that he is created for God".[3]

Such then would seem to be the knowledge about God which on Brunner's view is attainable through the revelation in creation to the man who has not Christian faith. It will be noted that here I say knowledge *about* and not knowledge of. This position seems to have been held by him from the days of early publications like *Erlebnis, Erkenntnis und Glaube* and *Philosophie und Offenbarung*, in both of which he vigorously repudiates the notion of a direct awareness of God.

Here then we have an exposition of the more negative tendency in Brunner's thought. But now we come to Brunner's doctrine of man,[4] which is a very central part of his teaching, and which might appear to contradict the material we have already examined, and might almost seem to justify John Baillie's phrase. "The Sense of the Presence of God". For here Brunner defines man as an essentially responsive, responsible being, a creature with a certain limited freedom, whose central characteristic is not his reason but his being-in-confrontation with the Eternal Thou. Man's being is a continuing answer

[1] *Op. cit.*, p. 310; E.T., p. 314-15.   [2] *Ibid.*, p. 311; E.T., p. 315.
[3] *Ibid.*, p. 321; E.T., p. 325.
[4] *Mensch im Widerspruch* gives this teaching most fully.

to the Eternal Word of creation which holds him in existence. Surely, we might say, a being who is essentially responsive stands in an I-Thou confrontation with the Creator who holds him in being. And Brunner believes that, even in his sin, man cannot escape this confrontation, this pattern of his existence. For where his response is not faith and love, it is still a response in rebellion and revolt, though that revolt may be hardly conscious.

Is there then indeed a contradiction here between two views in Brunner, or is the tension that we have described only one that expresses the very singular character of knowing and at the same time not-knowing which marks unbelieving man's reception of the general revelation? It can be shown at least that something of this tension is found not only in the theology of the Reformers but what is very much more important, in the thought of the New Testament. And may it not be true that while God speaks continually to man, man through disobedience, or lack of moral insight and perhaps partly through invincible ignorance, turns that dialogue into a monologue? Surely in Kant's *Religion Within the Limits of Reason Alone* and in his *Opus Postumum*, by which Brunner was all his life long fascinated, we have an example of this struggle in one great thinker. Here we see a long battle waged between the confession of a dialogue with the living God, and its misinterpretation as a monologue of the autonomous self.[1]

My own conclusion is that probably Brunner is not only expressing a tension to be found in the reality which confronts him, but at times involved in a certain degree of contradiction with himself. But I would be quite unwilling to give up his definition of man as essentially responsive created being, held in confrontation with the Eternal Thou. But if we do hold to this definition, we must acknowledge that here we are using language in a strange sense. For we will agree that when an answer is made in ordinary human discourse it must be made consciously to a person who confronts us. But Brunner's definition covers all men, including those who do not believe

[1] Brunner, *Gebot und Ordnungen*, p. 31; E.T., *The Divine Imperative*, p. 45-6.

in the reality of that God to whom their very being is here defined as an answer.

Yet this doctrine of man as an essentially responsive, responsible being, cannot be surrendered by those who hold that God is the One from whose grace and judgement man cannot escape. For this is a central part of the doctrine of man's existence in the image of God. In the writer's opinion this doctrine that all men stand in continual confrontation with God must be affirmed if we are to do justice to the biblical teaching about God's transcendence. And it appears further that writers like Bishop Robinson and William Hamilton, and indeed at times Dietrich Bonhoeffer, have been in danger of letting go their hold of something essential here. In Bonhoeffer's case it might be truer to say that there are at least certain sentences which he has written which on the face of them can only be interpreted in this sense as suggesting that modern man can really say "Goodbye" to God. This was certainly not the general intention of his theology, but these are sentences in his works to which others have unfortunately stuck themselves, like flies on flypaper.

But while affirming Brunner's teaching in general about man's relation to God, we may be tempted to ask whether he has not endeavoured to define too hard-and-fast limits of what is possible for God's revelation in places where the biblical revelation and Jesus Christ have never been heard of. Is there not a danger of our saying to God, "Thus far shalt Thou come and no further"? We do not cast doubt on the faith that in Christ we have the full revelation of the Father, and a revelation that not only fulfils but also reverses the teaching of other religions. Yet we may call in question what Brunner seems often to be saying—God is always in dialogue with every man, but no man who is not a Christian believer can be in dialogue with God. Non-Christians can and do know *about* God; but they can never know him.

For example where the context shows that he is speaking of the revelation in creation, Brunner says, "Even the man to whom God has not proclaimed his name, is not without a

D

knowledge of God, for a knowledge about the Creator is ineradicably associated with the creaturely existence of man. . . . Man left alone with nature and himself does not know the true God, because he does not know the God of revelation, the God whose nature it is to be the one who reveals and communicates himself."[1] Brunner then goes on to say that those who do not have the special revelation have only the idea of God, they are not in dialogue, but are isolated within the circle of the solitary self. And here I think he has gone too far. Barth said once, "Brunner is uncannily clear." Here, I believe, is a case in point. In order to have everything cut and dried, and quite perspicuous, he has actually landed himself in contradiction with a large and essential part of his own theology.

Might it not be more prudent and humbler to say that where a man standing outside the Hebrew-Christian revelation claimed to have been in real communion with God, in the I-Thou relationship with him, we might do well to reserve our judgement, and say, "It may have been so". The more that the things he said about God's revelation which he claimed to have received tallied with what we know of God in Christ, the more we might be inclined to believe him. And *that* even though we would continue to give all weight to such writers as Otto, Kraemer and Brunner himself, when they draw attention to fundamental differences which underlie superficial resemblances between other religions, such as Bhakti piety, and the Christian faith. It is one thing to deny the fundamental kinship between the teaching of such a religion and the revelation of God in Christ. It is another thing to deny that because of this difference the living God cannot, under such a mask, seek and find communion with them, as St. Paul says, in a slightly different context, "If haply they might feel after him and find him" (Acts 17:27).

There are two ways of approaching any claim to be in touch with God. There is the way taken by Karl Barth, who would put in each case the question "Is this God of whom you

[1] *Dogmatik* I, p. 126; E.T., p. 121.

speak, God the Father, Son and Holy Spirit?" and will come out, naturally in each case, with a triumphant "No!" There are, of course, cases where Barth's repudiation would be absolutely justified, where there were clearly present in the supposed revelation elements of the evil and demonic. But there is a second way possible. Instead of starting from below, where the water is already, as it were, muddied by human folly and sin, we may start from above, from the belief that God's original revelation underlies men's religions, though in greater or lesser degree they all caricature and distort it. Yet to start always from above thus would be if anything more disastrous than to start always from below, for then we would be free to regard all cults, however evil, as expressions of the divine grace.

This is a very mysterious and obscure area in which we must walk humbly and warily. If misconceptions of God were always to validate a radical denial that here God was known at all, who of us could claim to know him? It is clear that in human relationships some measure of communion can exist where there is imperfect knowledge. In human relationships, further, the action of a friend can so reveal to us his nobility of character that we must say, "I thought I knew him, but now I realise that I never really knew him until now". Could we then not say of people who claim to know God, but do not know him through Christ, "Yes, they may be in touch with him, but they will never really know him till they know his love for them in Christ"?[1]

I have tried in this chapter to deal with one source of our knowledge of God's transcendence, and one essential element in the nature of man, God's revelation in creation. I have tried to carry this discussion a few steps further than the point where Emil Brunner left it, and it may be that I have not made my case. I think, however, that there will be widespread

[1] This appears to me to have some kinship with a view expressed by Principal Alfred Hogg in *The Authority of the Faith*, Vol. I (The Tambaram series, O.U.P. (1939), pp. 102-25). "The Christian Attitude to Non-Christian Faith".

agreement with the position that only in the light of God's special revelation can this revelation in creation be rightly interpreted. And there will be even wider agreement that where this latter mode of God's transcendence is not understood, the nature of man himself is imperfectly apprehended.

CHAPTER IV

Transcendence in the Thought of
Paul Tillich

CLEARLY the theology of Paul Tillich cannot be ignored in any discussion of the transcendence of God, for his thought has been very influential in determining the recent course of the debate. Tillich has exercised this influence both directly through his own powerful writings and indirectly through the development, and some would say the distortion, which his thought has received at the hands of John Robinson, especially in Robinson's book *Honest to God*, and T. J. J. Altizer has claimed Tillich, his old teacher, as his spiritual father, a parentage which it was almost Tillich's latest act to disown.

Perhaps no thorough evaluation can be given of Robinson's position, unless some account has first been given of Tillich. In any case Robinson's verdict, in a central passage of *Honest to God*, is that Tillich's great contribution to theology is "the interpretation of transcendence in a way which preserves its reality while detaching it from the projection of supra-naturalism".[1] And he further cites Tillich as urging that his own interpretation is "more religious, because it is more aware of the unconditional character of the divine, than a theism that bans God into the supranatural realm".[2] (We note with amusement that when Tillich wrote these words, before 1951, the word "religious" was still an encomium, and not a term of derogation.)

The wide influence of Tillich and the confidence of his claims for his own system, as well as their emphatic endorse-ment by Robinson, make inevitable some discussion of his views in this study. Tillich is a baffling writer, but no student who takes some patience with him can fail to be impressed by his thought. His system is so closely morticed together, and

[1] *Honest to God*, p. 56.   [2] *The Protestant Era*, p. 92.

contains such profound insights, which often other theologians
seem to have missed, that the reader cannot fail to be impressed both by his encyclopaedic knowledge and his intellectual
power, and may begin to wonder whether, in spite of awaken-
ing grave doubts on matters of central importance, Tillich
may not have succeeded in making his case. It is clear that in a
study like this only a skeletal treatment will be possible, and
one which deals particularly with the one theme of transcendence and with other matters only as they group themselves
around this problem, I should like to say that most of the
question marks which I wish to set down are accompanied with
a due awareness of the fact that intellectually some of us do
not reach higher than his knees. Yet the questions must be
put, and what I knew of Paul Tillich personally, his friendly
and modest approach, and his intense respect for other people,
makes me feel that he would be the first to welcome all honest
attempts to make such criticisms, however strongly he might
dissent from and repudiate the conclusions of his critics.

Probably the best way of obtaining entrance to Tillich's
extremely close-knit system of thought, in pursuing our special
search for his doctrine of transcendence, will be by means of
a short study of two features of his system. The first is his
method of correlation, and the second is his ontological
philosophy.

First, then, the method of correlation. Tillich writes as a
theologian who is also a philosopher and a student of human
history and culture. He aims to stand on the boundary line
between Christian theology and the field of secular thought,
and to vindicate the relevance of faith to a world which has got
out of touch with the Christian gospel. This kind of assignment
has in the past been customarily allotted to Apologetics, which
at its best was a special department of theology concerned to
state the faith in relation to the questions, doubts and heresies
of contemporary man. But Tillich notes that for two reasons
this discipline has fallen into not undeserved discredit.[1] First,
it has often taken the weak and disgusting form of retreating

[1] *Systematic Theology*, I, p. 6.

before the advancing claims of scientific and historical knowledge, in order to find a place for God and his actions within
an otherwise completely calculable and "immanent" world.
Further, in its encounter with the world, apologetic has often
"sold the pass", so that its gospel was dissipated. As we shall
see, Tillich does not think that there should be a special
department of apologetic theology set over against dogmatics.
He attempts to do justice to the apologetic concern by means
of his own specific method of correlation.

Before he introduces this, he mentions three inadequate
methods of relating the Christian faith to man's spiritual existence; the supranaturalistic, the naturalistic, and the dualistic.
The first takes the Christian message to be a sum of revealed
truths which have fallen into the human situation like strange
bodies from a strange world. No mediation to the human situation is possible. The truths must create a new situation before
they can be received. This is something of a parody of Barth's
position. The second, the naturalistic method, is the reverse of
the first. It derives the Christian message from man's natural
state, unaware that human existence is the question, not the
answer. This was the position of extreme liberalism during the
last century. The third method is that of the Roman Church,
the dualistic method, which builds a supranaturalistic structure
on a natural substructure. Reason unaided can supply so much
truth about God. Here we have a legitimate field for apologetic
and natural theology. Above and beyond this we have the
truths of the Christian faith given by supernatural revelation.

Over against these three inadequate methods Tillich sets
his own method of correlation. He attempts to take up into
his systematic theology both the dogmatic elements, which
bear witness to the Christian revelation, and the element of
openness to the contemporary situation which was formerly
the characteristic interest of apologetic theology. This method
of correlation dictates the pattern of all his thinking, and the
shape of his three-volume *Systematic Theology*. In a word, it is
a system of questions and answers. The questions are derived

"by an analysis of human existence", while the theological answers are given on the strength of the Christian revelation. And Tillich endeavours to show that when human existence is analysed, man's crucial problems are disclosed. Then the Christian revelation is put forward as in each case the answer.

What does Tillich tell us about the analysis of the human situation? He tells us that it employs materials made available by man's creative self-interpretation in all realms of culture. The theologian organises these materials in relation to the answer given by the Christian message. In the light of this message he may make an analysis of existence more penetrating than that of most philosophers. Nevertheless, it remains a philosophical analysis.[1]

Now, the relation of philosophy to theology in Tillich is a difficult matter which I cannot here discuss at length. But it becomes clear that this analysis—in its nature as philosophical —is *not* theological; that is, it is not an analysis made in the light of the Christian revelation. In fact, the human situation does not have thrown on it, in this analysis, the light shed by the Incarnation, Cross and Resurrection of Christ. It is an analysis made on the basis of philosophy, which ought therefore to be convincing on rational grounds generally accepted. This remains the case in spite of the rather misleading words, "in the light of this message he may make an analysis of existence more penetrating than that of most philosophers".[2] The fact therefore remains that the questions, and the analysis from which they arise, have been formulated under the guidance of philosophy, and, in fact, under the guidance of a particular philosophy. And what this philosophy may be is a question which later will form a bridge from this first part of our discussion to the second, the discussion of Tillich's particular ontology. And we may well feel inclined to ask whether this method of correlation is really going to do justice to the authority of the Christian revelation any better than the old natural theology of liberalism, seeing that the revelation is apparently going to be limited to providing the answers to

[1] *Op. cit.*, I, p. 71.   [2] *Ibid.*, p. 71.

questions formulated for it by a special philosophy. Let it be said that Tillich's *intention* is not thus to gag or hamstring the Word of God, and there are a number of things in his theology which bear witness to this desire. But again, the logic of his own system appears to be too strong for him, and it is generally agreed that this extremely important section on the method of correlation is one of the weakest and most vulnerable places in his theology.

We note that the word "correlation" suggests an equal partnership between question and answer, so that the freedom of God to reveal his own message to man is unimpaired by this method. Yet, as we have already hinted, a closer examination does not confirm this impression. Kenneth Hamilton makes particularly telling use of quotations from Tillich to show what this equality in reality amounts to. He quotes the following sentence, "The answers implied in the event of revelation are meaningful only in so far as they are in correlation with questions concerning the whole of our existence, with existential questions".[1] "Without an understanding of 'being' and the 'power of being' it is impossible to speak meaningfully of grace."[2] To someone not acquainted with the close-knit Tillichian system, these words could only cause puzzlement. But what they really mean is that only those who are conversant with this system and the questions it formulates will be able to understand revelation or grace. Here Hamilton comments "The event of revelation—the content of the Christian gospel—cannot say anything for itself; it must merely answer such questions as are asked, supplying the kind of answer expected of it. This is to put the gospel in the position of a prisoner in the power of an inquisitor."[3]

One more quotation will suffice. Tillich writes, "In respect to content the Christian answers are dependent on the revelatory events in which they appear; in respect to form they are dependent on the structure of the questions they answer. God is the answer to the questions implied in human finitude.

---

[1] *Op. cit.*, I, p. 69.   [2] *Op. cit.*, p. 144.
[3] *The System and the Gospel*, p. 121.

This answer cannot be derived from the analysis of existence. However, if the notion of God appears in systematic correlation with the threat of non-being which is implied in existence, God must be called the infinite power of being which resists the threat of non-being. In classical theology this is being itself."[1]

Here we might ask whether the distinction between form and content can apply in this context. If I am restricted in the form which my answer takes, by the form of your questions, will there be any likelihood that I will be free to get across to you the content of what I want to say? And Hamilton further points out that while Tillich says that God as the answer to the question of human finitude cannot be derived from the analysis of existence, yet when he is forced to appear as the answer to a question proposed by the analysis of existence (i.e. Tillich's ontological philosophy), it is strange he appears as "the infinite power of being which resists the threat of non-being". Where did this notion appear from? Certainly not from the biblical revelation. In fact, both question and answer are produced from Tillich's ontology! We begin to ask ourselves if what we have here is not a metaphysical system parallel to that of Heidegger in the hands of Bultmann. Bultmann's plea is somewhat similar to Tillich's. Unless Christian faith is translated into the conceptuality provided by Heidegger, it is impossible for modern man to understand it. Yet, the systems of concepts which are by both proffered as necessary, are actually widely divergent, and we cannot help noting that fact with a certain amount of glee.

We must now pass to the second theme, the theme of Tillich's ontology, which we have been unable to avoid mentioning in passing.

I must now give an account, almost as brief as the previous section, of the ontology of Tillich. This is set forth in his section on "Being and the Question of God."[2] Here he is writing as a philosopher when he sets forth the ontological structure of

---

[1] *Systematic Theology*, I, p. 64.
[2] *Systematic Theology*, I, Part II, chap. 7.

being. Yet as his main purpose is theological, he does not claim that the elements and categories which he lists are a complete inventory, such as would be required in a philosophical work; he gives us only those which are the most important for theology. And it is clear from the rest of the three volumes how important this material is for him, for the whole work is an elaborate and often brilliant series of variations on the themes here mentioned for the first time. Any student of Tillich will therefore have to memorise and understand what is here set down.

Tillich tells us that no theology can escape the question of being. It is true that Kantian philosophy concentrated on the question of knowing, yet this problem cannot be studied in abstraction from the question of being; that is, epistemology cannot be studied in abstraction from ontology. If this is attempted, thoughtless prejudices and unconscious presuppositions about the nature of being will govern and distort the philosophical work. It is vain for positivists to reject this study on the grounds that it is metaphysical or ontological. For their own systems have ontological presuppositions to which they shut their own eyes. So the study of the nature of being is mandatory, and theology cannot escape it, though its interest is less theoretical and more practical, more existential, than that of philosophy. Theology studies being in so far as the latter is a matter of ultimate concern.

There are, Tillich tells us, four levels of ontological concepts. These concepts determine the nature of experience. All being which we can directly know presupposes a subject-object structure. All our knowing presupposes both someone who knows and something that is known. Another way of putting this is to say that it has a self-world pattern. We may call this a polar pattern. And this polar pattern is repeated on the second and third ontological levels, each of which presents us with three pairs of related and contrasted concepts. The second level is entitled "The Elements of Being", the contrasted concepts being Individualisation and Participation, Dynamics and Form, Freedom and Destiny. The third level is entitled the Characteristics of Being found in existence, and these are Being and non-Being, Infinite and Finite, Essence and Existence. The fourth level is that containing the categories according to which our experience is arranged, and of these, four have theological significance. They are Time and Space, Substance and Causality.

Tillich points out that since God is beyond all these polar structures, two most important consequences follow. The first is, that because God is above the polar opposites of essence and existence, we cannot say that he exists. This is a point which Tillich never tires of making. To say that God exists is to make of him one entity among others, an object, of however exalted a kind, within his own universe. This is idolatry. Tillich does not, of course, mean the same as Altizer and Pelz by his denial of the existence of God. What he means to say is perhaps, rather, that God is incomparable to all other realities, and in so far as this is his meaning, we would assent to his intention, while still claiming that it is necessary to speak of the existence of God, a matter which remains to be dealt with later in this chapter.[1]

The second consequence is even more important. It is this, that since God is outside the basic ontological structure of being which determines all that we can directly know, we cannot directly know him, our categories and polar concepts do not directly apply to him. In fact, they apply only symbolically to him. There is, however, one single exception to this veto; there is one thing that we can say non-symbolically of God, and that is that God is being-itself. Tillich writes: "The statement that God is being-itself is a non-symbolic statement. It does not point beyond itself. It means what it says directly and properly. If we speak of the actuality of God we first assert that he is not God if he is not being-itself. Of course religious assertions do not require such a foundation for what they say about God; the foundation is implicit in every religious thought concerning God. Theologians must make explicit what is implicit in religious thought and expression,

[1] P. 64.

and in order to do this, they must begin with the most abstract and completely unsymbolic statement which is possible, namely that God is being-itself or the absolute."[1]

At this point we must point out that for Tillich all statements of religious faith are symbolic, and this applies to Christian statements as well as those of other religions. What theologians must do is to interpret these symbols in the light of, and under the guidance of, the unsymbolic statement that God is being-itself.

Now Christian faith makes certain statements, e.g. that God is a Father, that he is love, that he is rightousness, that he hears and answers prayer. And Christian believers might feel inclined to agree with Tillich in his assertion, regarding what he says as pointing to the depth of mystery, and of transcendence, in God, recalling also the saying of Isaiah, "For my thoughts are not your thoughts, neither are your ways my ways, saith the Lord".[2]

But, as Hamilton has pointed out, "It is one thing to deny that God can be defined in terms of human experience, and quite another to affirm that he can be properly defined in other terms available to us. Tillich offers a description of the divine by means of which genuine deity may be tested; the God who is really God is that which precedes the subject-object structure of being. . . . The God of Scripture is indeed prior to all beings. . . . Yet what makes God prior is the truth that Lordship belongs to him. He is not called Lord because he is known to be the necessary precondition for that grade of being which things in heaven and in earth demonstrably possess."[3]

Thus Tillich's ontology claims to show what we can say clearly and directly about God, and so to provide a criterion by which we may positively and negatively evaluate all religious statements about him, including Christian and biblical ones. The task of theology, he declares, is to evaluate the "religious substance of these myths, rites, and symbols".[4] Tillich believes that the Bible bears witness to real, necessary

[1] *Systematic Theology*, I, pp. 264-5. [2] Isaiah 55:8.
[3] Hamilton, *op. cit.*, p. 83. [4] *Systematic Theology*, I, p. 19

and saving revelation, because owing to our estranged existence in the world the essential unity of man with God has been broken. He also believes that through this real yet symbolic revelation God acts in healing this estrangement. But the estrangement is not so radical as to break the link with the Divine Being which makes possible and guarantees the Tillichian ontology. And that is why Christianity must submit to the theological interpretation which uses this ontology.

It must now be our task to look briefly at the place where this ontology is suspended, as it were by a hook hanging from a ring in the heavenly ceiling. Is there not something insecure here, so that a more adequate picture would be that of an Indian conjurer performing the rope trick, casting it up into the air and then climbing up it out of sight, where the true solution of the puzzle may be that the spectators have been lulled into a hypnotic trance and think they see what is in fact not there?

Tillich tells us that the only thing we can say directly about God is that he is being-itself, or that he is the ground of the ontological structure of being without being subject to this structure. Or that he is the structure, that is, that he has the power of determining the structure of everything that has being. Or again that he is the infinite abyss and ground of being. But are not all these statements, in so far as meaning can be attached to them, themselves taken from the world that we know directly, and therefore, because they are applied beyond it, symbolic?

There appears further to have been discussion between Tillich and others since the first volume of the *Systematic Theology* was written,[1] for in the early pages of the second volume he tells us so, and he appears as a result to have modified his formulation of his non-symbolic and direct statement about the ground of being. He tells us that there is a point where a non-symbolic assertion about God must be made, and adds "There is such a point, namely the statement that

[1] Published 1953.

everything we say about God is symbolic. Such a statement is about God, and it is not symbolic."[1] But surely the statement is now no longer about God, it is about statements about God, who has now retreated entirely behind symbols, leaving no ontological criterion by means of which we can directly evaluate them.

Now, at an earlier stage of the argument Tillich was eager to point out that symbols must not be decried as "merely symbols", for a symbol has a positive ontological relation to that which it symbolises. In relation to the religious symbols used about God, he tells us that they have a double character; they are inadequate because they use the subject-object structure which he transcends. But they also have a positive relation to him; they do refer to him, though inadequately, because he is the ground of the whole universe in which they are rooted. But surely it would be more logical to say that if we base ourselves on reason alone, the infinite ground of being is really an X about which nothing can be said. If we conceive of God merely as the infinite ground of being, must we not say that his relationship to the universe is a wholly enigmatic one? If this is true, then we have one more indication that the Tillichian ontology has collapsed, leaving us with philosophical uncertainty. The concept of the infinite ground of being is in itself an empty one.

I believe that in fact the symbols—for example the symbols of Fatherhood, Lordship and Creatorhood—do refer to God. But this not because he is immediately known as the infinite ground of being, but because he has revealed himself to us through these symbols which he has chosen as fitting. And in so revealing himself he gives to them a partially new meaning, so that they are able to express his nature and his attributes to us. The justification of the symbols is thus not philosophical but a result of the special historical revelation.

The collapse of Tillich's ontology, with its claim to make at least one unsymbolic statement about God, has an important consequence which may here be pointed out. This is that the

[1] *Systematic Theology*, II, p. 10.

veto imposed by Tillich and John Robinson on talk about the existence of God will have to be lifted. Towards the end of his book on *The Existence of God* Helmut Gollwitzer has two sections entitled "The Necessity of Is-Propositions" and "The Inadequacy of Is-Propositions"—in their application to God. Gollwitzer draws our attention to the fact that when we talk of God's existence we do not mean exactly the same thing as when we refer to any other existence. Here he makes the further crucially important observation, "If our earlier assertion is correct, that *all* our concepts are anthropomorphic, then there is no point in prohibiting specifically the use of such concepts as 'existence' and 'reality' with reference to God. Such a prohibition would be a sign that we still thought it possible to distinguish between concepts as in themselves adequate or inadequate in speaking of God. Instead of that we must reflect on the transformation which takes place in the concept of existence when God becomes its subject."[1]

There is little doubt that Bishop Robinson has here followed the lead of Tillich, with his claim to non-symbolic knowledge of God. The thrust of Robinson's polemic against the "God out there" (whom he describes as mythological) is precisely an attack on the concept not only of God's up-thereness, but also on that of God's existence,[2] in favour of his own concept of transcendence as the depth of being. Our answer will be that all these concepts are symbolic, but that there is special danger in a day when it is claimed that God is dead, of denying his existence, when the same (inadequate) grounds can be adduced to object to any theological statement whatsoever.

These reflections of Gollwitzer's could give a real liberation to those who feel that since Robinson has spoken we may no longer talk or think of the existence of God.

It is impossible even in a brief discussion like this to disregard a very important, though short, essay by Tillich upon this

---

[1] *Existenz Gottes*, p. 164; E.T., p. 204.
[2] See *Honest to God*, esp. pp. 48-9. "The theist is concerned to argue the existence of such a Being. . . . But the way of thinking we are seeking to expound is not concerned to posit such a Being at all."

theme of the divine transcendence.[1] Here Tillich both states the case against himself with an extreme frankness, and then tries to answer it. He first describes the thought of the Bible as formulating with special sharpness that personalism which is common to religion.

"The God who is unconditioned in power, demand, and promise is the God who makes us completely personal, and who consequently is completely personal in our encounter with him."[2] "Nothing seems to contradict the ontological concept of 'being' more than this reciprocity between God and man. How can a being act upon being itself? How can being itself be mutually related to any particular being? How can a being influence the ground of being in which and out of which it lives?"[3]

Yet, Tillich continues, within biblical religion itself there are essential elements which make it necessary for us to ask the ontological question. "The ultimate concern of the believer is concern about that which is really ultimate, and therefore the ground of his being and meaning. . . . As a believer he is not concerned with ontological research, but he is concerned with truth, and this means with ultimate reality. . . . Faith in anything which has only preliminary reality is idolatry."[4]

I would entirely agree with this claim that the faith of the Christian would be idolatry if he did not claim that the God whom he worships is the most real one. This is an essential element in biblical religion. But I would dissent from Tillich's assumption that this assertion of faith necessitates the adoption of Tillich's ontology. For this ontology entails the claim that man has an intellectual grasp of being which depends upon a hidden unity between himself and absolute being that enables him to make non-symbolic affirmations about God.

Faith indeed claims to make assertions about reality, and the theologian is bound to attempt in some measure to say what this implies. He does so by trying to relate his knowledge of God to other knowledge. This is a task of apologetics, and it is

---

[1] *Biblical Religion.*
[2] *Ibid.*, p. 27.
[3] *Op. cit.*, p. 31.
[4] *Op. cit.*, p. 54.

a never-finished task which makes use of what concepts it can. But Tillich has not the right to assume, as he does, that all apologetic theology should accept his ontology, for in our opinion such acceptance means that the loyalty to Christian revelation comes second to the acceptance of Tillich's particular philosophy of being.

If, however, we can believe that out of the darkness and mystery the final reality has approached, and has addressed us by name, revealing himself to us, then we may well admit the symbolic nature of the concepts in which that revelation is clothed, acknowledging that here they are not being used in exactly the sense that they bear in our daily life with one another. But we can trust that the symbols are true, because God himself is true, in the sense in which the Bible uses that word of him, and desires, not to deceive us, but to communicate himself to us.

We have now come to the end of the space at our disposal for dealing with Paul Tillich's thought on transcendence. If we ask ourselves to which does he owe an ultimate loyalty, to the biblical revelation or to his own ontology, we shall, I think be forced to agree that the latter alternative is the one chosen, though he struggles very hard, as it were, against the grain of his own system in order to do justice to the biblical revelation.

A fuller and more thorough study, made from the point of view here represented, would have involved taking the essential concepts of divine transcendence as given in the biblical revelation, and other concepts related closely to them, such as the concept of prayer, and examining how each one of these fares in the theology of Tillich. Gollwitzer has done this in relation to the subject of prayer,[1] and Nels Ferré has done it with reference to the I-Thou relationship of man to God.[2] At the end of each examination we would have to ask ourselves, "Does Tillich's theology do justice to this essential strand in the biblical teaching?" It might well be that his terminology

[1] *Existenz Gottes*, p. 134; E.T., p. 167.
[2] Ferré, *Scottish Journal of Theology*, Sept. 1957, "Three critical issues in Tillich's Theology".

was quite different from the biblical terminology, and yet essentially faithful to the Bible for all that! If we were satisfied that justice was being done by Tillich to the biblical revelation, then we would have to ask the further question, "Is the justice done to this concept logically compatible with the structure of Tillich's system?" It is probable that the results of such inquiries, carefully and disinterestedly pursued over a period, will decide the future of Tillich's influence and theological reputation.

CHAPTER V

Transcendence in the Thought of Werner Pelz and John Robinson

WERNER PELZ was mentioned briefly in the first chapter, but it may be worth our while to consider his writing a little less superficially, as an example of the "God is Dead" theology, which in my opinion has importance rather as an irritant than as a serious theological contribution. Further, I have so far seen no criticisms of Mr. Pelz, while van Buren has been dealt with faithfully and in great detail by Eric Mascall, and T. J. J. Altizer has been criticised uproariously and I think effectively by Robert McAfee Brown in a long review article in *Theology Today*.[1]

This criticism will be confined to what Pelz has written in his book *God is no More* on the subject of transcendence—if, indeed an outright denial of transcendence can be called a treatment of the theme. It should be noted that when Pelz is not dealing with theology he often writes with great sensitivity, originality and wisdom.

One of the favourite quotations of the new theologians of the left is the Johannine saying of Christ, "He that hath seen me hath seen the Father". Johannes Körner quotes it, John Robinson quotes it, van Buren quotes it, and Pelz quotes it. In the case of the last two men one may be tempted to say that the exegesis is made in the hope that if they can get their interpretation of this passage accepted, they can get away with anything.[2]

Let us recall for a moment the context in which this verse stands, the context of the fourteenth chapter of St. John, Jesus' words to his disciples, "Let not your heart be troubled, ye believe in God, believe also in me. In my Father's house

[1] *Theology Today*, July 1966, Vol. XXIII, No. 2, pp. 279-90.
[2] See Appendix B, p. 110.

are many mansions. . . . I am the way, the truth, and the life, no man cometh unto the Father but by me. He that hath seen me hath seen the Father; how sayest thou then, Shew us the Father."[1]

Here, as uniformly in the four Gospels, and not least in St. John, the background motif is the transcendence of the Father. The Son's whole will is to do the Father's will. Against this background must be read the words, "He that hath seen me hath seen the Father". Jesus is not truly seen unless he is seen as the way and door to the Father, though he is not a door that we can close and leave behind us.

What does Mr. Pelz make of this? He says that what Jesus means is this, "He who has seen me has seen God. Why do you still ask for more?"[2] It is still possible to believe that Pelz means what the evangelist meant. But when Pelz writes the following words, "There is no God but Jesus, says the author of St. John's gospel, because his words more than any other words refresh us, guide and gather us, resuscitate us"; how this can be squared with the clear meaning of the passage which Pelz claims to be interpreting, is anyone's guess. How can it be squared with the obvious sense of "No man hath seen God at any time, the only begotten son of the Father he hath declared him"? For Pelz God is merely Jesus' dream, and the Kingdom of God merely the realisation of man's latent possibilities. "In so far as he lived his hope . . . he had the right to say, I and my hope are one, he who has seen me has seen my hope."[3] (Here obviously we have a reference made by Pelz to "I and the Father are one", and "He that hath seen me hath seen the Father.")

It is interesting that Mr. Pelz paints in at one point a background of Old Testament history which might seem to augur well for his doctrine of divine transcendence. "According to the Old Testament which, so far as we know, was the only book that Jesus knew well, forgiveness belongs to Yahweh alone. . . . Yahweh *forgives* by calling man into a purpose, a

---

[1] John 14:1, 2, 6 and 9b.   [2] *God is no More*, p. 67.
[3] *Op. cit.*, p. 109.

hope beyond that by which he had been content to live. He coaxes them to listen to the commandments which will make new men out of slaves. . . . When the prophets call the Israelites into renewed obedience, trust and hope, they point to the archetypal pattern of Yahweh's work. . . . The people of Yahweh are encouraged to hope in him because he was and is the awakener of their hopes, to trust in him because he has vindicated his trustworthiness. . . . Yahweh's forgiveness is his persistent calling and recalling into hope and trust and love."[1]

Pelz now tells us that Jesus accepts and sharpens the Old Testament view. So far, it would appear, so good. But now he writes, "The New Testament understands unbelief, not as immorality, but as inability to believe in our own opportunities. We are sinners because we refuse to follow our hope, to trust our desires, to obey our vision." What has happened? God has disappeared, sunk without trace. He has been replaced by "our opportunities". So that we now have the paradox—if it is no more—of forgiveness without God, unbelief as sin, without a God to believe in. Jesus' love for the Father becomes his devotion to his hope (for which no grounds are offered) that men can and will respond to his challenge, throw away all security and give themselves to their neighbour. He who does this becomes Christ to his neighbour. It is one thing to say that God is our hope, but a very different thing to say that our hope is God.[2] Here is salvation, not from God, but through pulling our boots on. Jesus is the man who challenges us to do this, and God is dissipated into the human I-Thou encounter. When Mr. Pelz at the beginning of his book pleads that we must not come to the gospel with our minds full of presuppositions, but allow the words of Jesus and the words about Jesus make their own impact upon us, we agree with conviction.[3] Our minds must be open, and free for the purpose of the writers, and for the Holy Spirit to make his own impact upon us, without any pre-understanding which would make us insensitive to this impact.

[1] Op. cit., p. 114.   [2] Op. cit., p. 109.   [3] Op. cit., pp. 13-15.

But it is all a blind; this is precisely what he does not himself do; his interpretation is an impudent correction of the clear meaning of the text. It is noticeable that writers like Pelz and van Buren cannot quite make up their minds whether they will confess that their interpretation is neither that interpretation which the biblical writers put upon their own writings, nor in the case where Jesus is in question, the meaning which he intended his words to have. Sometimes Jesus is made to talk Pelzese, or van Burenese, at others we are told what Jesus really meant to say, and would have said if he had known with Werner Pelz that God is dead, or if he had sat with Paul van Buren at the feet of Frederick Ayer, and knew in consequence that "God" was a sound without significance. We know what are the reasons for van Buren's denial of transcendence. It is a little less clear why Pelz has come to the conclusion that "God is no more." It would appear that he has succumbed to the Freudian criticism that God is no more than the projection of the superego, the repressive conscience. All the way through his book he goes on misinterpreting Jesus' sayings in ways which deny the divine transcendence. Once only is the question of God not regarded as settled in the negative sense. And this is where he says, "If there be a God—and we have to admit that Jesus thought so—we can find him only in our neighbour, when our neighbour has become a friend."[1] It is a little difficult to understand why gnostics like this should wish to climb upon the Christian bandwaggon at all.

In my second chapter I made the suggestion that in examining every doctrine of divine transcendence we should ask whether the thinker under consideration felt that his ultimate loyalty was to the Christian revelation of God, or to some other, philosophical understanding of his transcendence. In the case of Werner Pelz, where there is a total denial of that transcendence, that question does not, of course, arise. Here there is no real openness to the Christian revelation, and consequently no loyalty to it.

Now we come to the second of our writers to be considered

[1] *Op. cit.*, p. 33.

in this chapter, the Bishop of Woolwich. The Bishop is a much more complex figure, and his intentions are much more positive. As I indicated in my last chapter, it was Robinson who set the ball rolling in Britain, or at least kicked off in the most recent match of the context. For Kenneth Hamilton is quite right when he points out that this debate about God's transcendence has been going on now for many years.

The views propounded in *Honest to God* have been discussed so many times of late, and in such detail, that there is something of a sense of weariness in returning to the theme, but it is really not possible to deal with the theme of God's transcendence today and pass Robinson over. I shall look first at his book, *Honest to God*, and then go on to deal with part of the discussion in his second book, *The New Reformation?* We know that Dr. Robinson recognises the central importance of the problem of transcendence, and indeed explicitly claims that he is not concerned to substitute an immanent for a transcendent deity, but rather to "validate the idea of transcendence for modern man".[1] He is therefore not a wholly congenial bedfellow for Werner Pelz.

I shall now in the briefest way recapitulate the argument of the first part of *Honest to God* to refresh the reader's memory. Robinson starts off with the Bible's picture of "A God up there", which we have learnt to take not literally but metaphorically. Now comes stage number two, and Robinson points out the hazardous nature of the enterprise to which he invites us. The stage we have now reached is that where the idea of a God even spiritually or metaphysically "out there" may have to be surrendered. This naturally, he says, causes perturbation among the people of faith. " . . . The idea of a God spiritually or metaphysically 'out there' dies very much harder" (than the idea of a God 'up there' literally). " . . . For it *is* their God, and they have nothing to put in its place". In fact, "it is the God of our own upbringing and conversation, the God of our fathers and of our religion who is under attack. Every one of us lives with some mental picture of a God 'out

---

[1] *Honest to God*, p. 44.

there', a God who 'exists' above and beyond the world he made, a God 'to' whom we pray, and to whom we 'go' when we die."[1] Yet, Robinson continues, there are signs that we are reaching the point at which the whole conception of a God 'out there' has served us so well since the collapse of the three-decker universe, is itself becoming more of a hindrance than a help. Of course, to give up the idea of a being meta- phorically 'out there' will appear to many to be an outright denial of God. Yet suppose that this conception of God is nothing more than an idol—a projection in the Freudian sense, an illusion—and that we are being called on to live without it at all!

Robinson now raises the question whether this biblical view of the world, which he calls unashamedly supranaturalist and mythical, is essential to Christianity. "Even when we have refined away what we should regard as the crudities and literalism of this construction, we are still left with what is essentially a mythological picture of God and his relation to the world."[2] "Is it necessary for the biblical faith to be ex- pressed in terms of this world-view, which in its way is as primitive philosophically as the Genesis stories are primitive scientifically?"[3] Robinson is convinced that the whole biblical conception of transcendence, not merely the "crudities and literalism of this construction", is expendable, and that such a reconstruction as he proposes is both possible and necessary. In the following chapters he outlines his rebuilding project. In short, it is a project which regards God as the infinite ground and depth of being—a term which is, of course, taken from Tillich.

At this point I would like to point out one curious difference between Robinson and Tillich. For Tillich, God can and must be described in non-symbolic language as the ground and depth of being, but the symbols of the Christian faith, God as person, God as Father—in short, all the biblical concepts of personal religion—remain necessary because of the estrange- ment of man's being under the conditions of existence. Here

[1] *Op. cit.*, p. 14.   [2] *Op. cit.*, p. 32.   [3] *Op. cit.*, p. 33.

Tillich is far more Christian than Robinson, who in this passage, at least, is suggesting that these symbols be swept away as "more of a hindrance than a help". Here is an example of the danger which men incur when they do not understand a theology, and try to make a new one by taking shreds of this thinker and patches of the next and putting the one to the other.

Robinson's attempt first to describe, and then to vindicate, his new projection of transcendence is extremely confused and irritating. We cannot help feeling that the conception of transcendence which he repudiates is a man of straw, or even an Aunt Sally. We are reminded of Calvin's jibes at popular misconceptions of the persons of the Trinity being like nothing so much as three marmosets. Further, it is Robinson's habit not logically to develop one line of thought, but to pursue an erratic course from one quotation to another. Confronted by him the reader feels like a man trying to wrestle with a naked opponent covered in soap.

What does Robinson mean when he declares that God is the infinite ground and depth of being? Let us hear what he has to say. Drawing the contrast between the new projection and the biblical one, of a Person out there, Robinson writes "But the way of thinking we are seeking to expound is not concerned to posit. . . . such a Being at all. In fact, it would not naturally use the phrase '*a* personal God'; for this in itself belongs to an understanding of theology and of what theological statements are about which is alien to it. For this way of thinking, to say that 'God is personal' is to say that 'reality at its very deepest level is personal', that personality is of *ultimate* significance in the constitution of the universe. . . . A statement is 'theological' not because it relates to a particular Being called 'God', but because it asks *ultimate* questions about the meaning of existence: it asks what, at the level of *theos*, at the level of its deepest mystery, is the reality and significance of our life."[1]

Now with Robinson's intention I would agree, in so far as he is endeavouring to do justice to the fact that God does not

[1] *Op. cit.*, pp. 48, 49.

exist in the same manner as other beings exist. As Gollwitzer says, "Is" propositions are both inadequate and necessary in relation to him. But it will be noticed that in his effort to expound a new projection Robinson has only succeeded in translating statements about God into statements about something else, the reality and significance of our life. The words quoted above are pure cotton-wool, even though, or perhaps because, their inspiration is Paul Tillich. Here God has disappeared in a cloud of self-understanding in a manner that would horrify Rudolf Bultmann. St. John would have said, not that knowing God could be defined exhaustively as knowing what "at the level of theos is the reality and significance of our life", but that life could only find its reality and significance in the knowledge of God.

Robinson continues "Belief in God is . . . the well-nigh incredible trust that to give ourselves to the uttermost in love is not to be confounded but to be 'accepted', that Love is the ground of our being, to which we ultimately 'come home' ". Here the language of personal encounter is concealed, though with imperfect success. Can the ground of our being love us? If to give ourselves to the uttermost in love is to be accepted, then we may well ask, by what, or by whom, are we accepted? By the deepest levels of reality, or by a Thou who confronts us, and whom we must call a Person? Robinson betrays his discomfort by placing the words "come home" and "accepted" in inverted commas, as if they could only be understood metaphorically. But must they not be taken literally? And if Love is spelt with a capital "L" does this not indicate the personal, Thou-character of its source?

This discussion of passages in *Honest to God* must come to an end, for Robinson-hunting can become very tedious to the hearer or reader, as the attempt is made to smoke the Bishop out, sentence by sentence, from fox-hole after fox-hole. But it would appear from the above examination that his attempt to construct a new model of transcendence to replace the biblical one, has broken down. The biblical notion which had been expelled by the front door has crept in at the back door with the use of I-Thou language to describe God. Yet Robinson has not realised this, for he asks us to believe that the criterion by which all "out there" language about God should be judged is this, that the God we turn to should be "the God and Father of our Lord Jesus Christ", and chooses as one of his favourite illustrations of living faith the great passage in Romans 8 which tells us that nothing in life or death can separate us from the love of God which is in Jesus Christ our Lord. This is "out there" language *par excellence*. To put the cap on it, Dr. Robinson in a later contribution[1] tells us that when confronted by the question "Do you pray to the Depth of your being?" answered "I pray to God as Father". What is necessary for the Bishop in his own prayers, cannot, surely, be expendable on such easy terms in theology as he assumes in *Honest to God*.

It is clear that for Robinson's own theology depth-language cannot supply all the necessary categories; here those which are demanded are those which we saw Brunner eliciting from the biblical revelation, God's lordship, over-ruling, the creator-creature relationship, God's holiness and love. But the trouble is that Dr. Robinson is unable to benefit by his own failures, for his thinking is not sufficiently clear for him to realise what is happening to his arguments as he develops them. Some recent writing of his shows that while he has now (reportedly) given up his use of the conception of God as the infinite depth of being, his grasp of the meaning of transcendence is as precarious as ever. The evidence for this is given in an Appendix to his valuable and stimulating book *The New Reformation?* Here I shall enter into debate with that Appendix (No. 1) only in so far as what he says there throws light upon this matter of divine transcendence.

Robinson begins the Appendix[2] with the startling question whether a truly contemporary person must not be an atheist. But it soon appears that his real meaning is that Christians who are mentally alive in the modern world must have felt

---

[1] *The Honest to God Debate*, p. 262.
[2] *The New Reformation*, pp. 107-21.

the pressure of contemporary doubt upon their spirits. Faith today is, he tells us, a thing that will for more and more be possible only on the far side of the atheist critique. Let us then, Robinson continues, expose ourselves to three thrusts of modern atheism against the Christian faith as it has been traditionally understood. God is intellectually superfluous, God is emotionally dispensable, God is morally intolerable. Cumulatively, these thrusts appear to be fatal, at least in the eyes of an increasing number of people. This result Robinson describes as the death of God. Yet there appears to be a resurrection of God, "out the other side". Though intellectually superfluous, emotionally dispensable, morally intolerable, yet he will not let us go. Thus far Robinson.

But our question then arises, who has died, and who is resurrected? Do the objections that were so fatal to the God whom they killed, apply to the God who is resurrected? Either they do, or they do not. In the first case, then surely he is nothing more than an emotional left-over of whom it is not easy all at once to rid ourselves. Or they do not—and I think I see in Robinson's argument signs that he believes that the God who in his view is resurrected, is not vulnerable to these thrusts. But whether this God is near enough to the transcendent God of Christian faith as hitherto known, to be worthy of the same title, is another matter. If in the end he proves not to be worthy of the name, then God will indeed have died, and divine transcendence will have collapsed along with him.

Now to come to closer grips with the argument. The first thrust of atheism is that God is intellectually superfluous, and Robinson quotes Laplace's famous words, "I have no need of that hypothesis". To bring in God to fill the as yet unexplained gaps in our scientific or historical knowledge is a hopeless project, and Robinson quotes Bonhoeffer's words that "in the scientific field and in the field of control, in human affairs generally, God is being edged out of the picture". Bonhoeffer concludes that though the apologists have now surrendered on all secular problems, "it is still claimed that the so-called ultimate problems remain", "on which only 'God' can furnish an answer'. . . . "But what if one day they no longer exist as such, if they too can be answered without 'God?' "[1]

Here, surely, two very different issues are being confused by Bonhoeffer and Robinson. It is clear that the "God of the gaps" argument is doomed from the start, though it was urged by Aquinas. But now we find that the valid attack on the argument of the gaps is being illegitimately enlarged to justify something quite different, all attemps of men to get along without God. Bonhoeffer includes in the ultimate problems which men may some day solve without God, the problems of death and guilt. Here I believe that Christians must stand fast, and declare that such answers are illusions. Certainly Bonhoeffer was right in his disgust with the "snuffling" apologists who love to pry out men's weaknesses so as to reduce them to despair, in order to proffer God to them as the answer. As Bonhoeffer says, man is to be sought also in his strength, in the midst of his life. Yet to do justice to the facts, we must acknowledge both the grandeur and the misery of man. And we must affirm that the problem of guilt remains, and if ever scientific progress and the growth of the range of human autonomy were to succeed in removing it, then not only the Christianity of the "snufflers" but the Christianity of the Bonhoeffers and the Robinsons would be snuffed out, and man would have saved himself. Christians are committed to claiming that positivist or idealist philosophies cannot do more than blind men for a while to the problem of guilt; they cannot really solve it.

It seems that in the first thrust of atheism, what has happened is this. Man's dominion over the world, of which the Bible speaks, which is surely celebrated in the phrase "man's coming of age"—has been illogically enlarged to an illegal declaration of independence over against God. One element in the image of God in man has been illegitimately over-emphasised so as to destroy the still more important dignity, promise and judgement involved in the total image. The God from whom man could with impunity cut himself adrift would

[1] *Letters and Papers from Prison*, pp. 145-6.

no longer be the transcendent God of biblical revelation. He would indeed be dead.

The second thrust of atheism does not here call urgently for discussion, so I shall omit it, though I believe that if there were time I could prove that in dealing with it Robinson's failure to do justice to the transcendence of God is shown also.

We shall pass on to the third thrust, that "God is morally intolerable". Here we come to the very centre of the problem of evil, and we must confess that none of us has an adequate answer to it, for we all from time to time feel the pressure of this great mystery, and any faith that we have come to in spite of its challenge is one that has to be won time and time again by a struggle against suffering and doubt.

It seems, however, that Dr. Robinson overstates his case when he says "Religion is disgusting. . . . To push off evil on to God simply makes him into a devil—and in any case represents a cowardly evasion."[1] At this point it is extremely difficult to know what our friend means. Is he suggesting that an easy answer given by us, by simply "passing the buck" to God, is blasphemous? In that case we would entirely concur with what he says—this is a habit which people have of describing other people's disasters, not their own usually—as being "all for the best." Or is Robinson saying—and I suspect that this is what he means—that the very idea of conceding that in some way God must be responsible for evil even if it only be that he is Lord over a world in which it can exist— that this is unthinkable blasphemy? We may grant the truth of what he says, that people today look for natural causes, instead of ascribing events direct to God, yet this does not necessarily imply that God has no freedom to guide events, or responsibility for things that happen. We can ease the moral problem caused by belief in this responsibility, we can do it in various ways which I have no space to discuss here. But it would seem that Robinson can do it only by declaring that God has no responsibility for evil, because secondary causes have taken over complete control. But can such a God

[1] *Op. cit.*, p. 113.

be more than a phantom? What has happened to his transcendence? How can Robinson square such a belief as this with
what appear to be the two central tenets of his working faith,
first, that Jesus is a window through into uttermost reality
("He that hath seen me hath seen the Father") and, secondly,
"I am persuaded that nothing can separate us from the love
of God which is in Christ Jesus our Lord"? A God who can
prevent such separation must be one who is in control of the
course of events.

At the close of his Appendix Robinson has profound things
to say about God as revealed in the suffering of the cross, as
one who does not stand aloof from human suffering and sin,
but takes responsibility for it. Yet Robinson at the same time
repudiates the absentee God who might have rescued Jesus from
suffering and did not do so. The "God who could have sent
'twelve legions of angels' and did not is exposed" he tells us,
"as the God who failed even his son. The obituary read by
the atheist is valid, even if sometimes shrill."[1] But if the God
to whom Jesus prayed on the cross, failed him there, and was
thus exposed as a God whose unreality was proved by that
failure—and if Robinson's words mean anything, they must
mean this—then what we are left with is a Jesus who in some
way is of ultimate significance because of his character and
death, but the transcendent God has disappeared. And this is
the position, as near as may be, of van Buren and Pelz. It
seems to me that this reading of Bonhoeffer, whom Robinson
thinks he is here following, leads to a complete loss of the
transcendent God, and this is entirely opposed to Robinson's
own avowed position.

This result, in my opinion, entirely vindicates Kenneth
Hamilton's earlier criticism of *Honest to God*, which runs as
follows "The Robinsonian theology promises a revolution, but
does not produce a coherent manifesto. At the same time, its
very confusions are illuminating. Its attempt to bring heaven
down to a dimension of earth shows the strength of the contemporary trend to establish an anti-supernaturalist theology

[1] *Op cit.*, p. 121.

of meaningfulness. And its final falling back upon traditional language indicates that Christian faith cannot simply be detached from a 'supernatural frame of reference.' "[1] All that I can say of this recent Appendix is that it shows Robinson more hopelessly adrift than ever he was in his first book.

It will be recalled that at an early stage of this book I proposed to ask one question each time a new writer was discussed: "Where does this man place his ultimate loyalty? Is his main intention to be faithful to the biblical revelation, or to a natural theology which he believes to give him a more sure criterion of truth, and which will accommodate his teaching to the current contemporary opinion?"

In Robinson's case the question is unusually hard to answer because the writing is so confused. There is undoubtedly in him a desire to be true to the Christian revelation. Even when he desires to give a new projection for transcendence, this is surely the case. But he is not a lucid enough thinker to realise what is happening, and what decisions face him, so that a clear-sighted choice is never possible. But there is no doubt in my mind that in his attempt to define Christian faith so that almost anyone who has had an experience of depth is acclaimed as a fellow-Christian, he is succumbing to the temptation of following another gospel than the Christian one, generous though even here I believe his motives to be.

At this point in my study I would like to add a note relating to the Death of God theologies, on whose fringe Robinson stands. For some time I have been convinced that this title is a misnomer. It is not the death of God which faces us, but the threatened death of man, and of the Church. Much of what Robinson says is false when said of God, but true when said of man and of the Church.

This surely is the main thrust in Vahanian's writing. For him the death of God means the loss of man's sense of God. In his *Religion and the Christian Faith* Hendrik Kraemer speaks of this in a fascinating passage. Talking of man's continual wavering between insecurity and security, which has always

[1] *Revolt against Heaven*, p. 37.

F

hitherto accompanied his awareness of God, he says, "In this light it becomes a still more disturbing riddle that as far as religion is concerned, modern man is seemingly so largely atrophied. This demands an extensive and penetrating treatment. Is the *cor inquietum* dying out? . . . [Here, of course, Kraemer is quoting from St. Augustine's famous statement, 'Thou hast made us for Thyself, and our heart is restless until it find its rest in thee'.] Is Luther's statement 'Man has either God or an idol' no longer applicable? . . . Is it the last and most dangerous form of escape from God to feign death, as the animals do?"[1] Personally, I believe that this new apathy is not a permanent character of the new man, any more than that God's image in him has been obliterated by his coming of age.

Thus I have a feeling in reading Robinson, Altizer and others that what they are saying is bad theology, but would be valid if translated into terms of the doctrine of man or the doctrine of the church. They combat as pernicious the notion of a dualism between God and his world. We have seen in what sense there must be a dualism between God and the world. But there is a pernicious dualism *on earth*, and that is between the Church and the world. Only through reimmersion in the world can the Church find the true God, not because he is the depth of being, but because he is the Lord of both Church and world, and has commissioned the Church to serve the world. Why is there this gap between Church and world? Because, as men like Peter Berger and Gibson Winter remind us, the Church is in grave danger of worshipping, not the living God, but the pressures of current opinion and the need for security. In so far as it does this, the God it worships will not be the living God, but a projection of human values and needs—a mere idol. No wonder that this God seems to lose substance and reality more and more as the years pass. He is only a reflection of the sick Church. We shall find the living God again only in so far as in obedience to him we turn to the world.

[1] *Op. cit.*, p. 313.

I do not think that man will die, or that the Church will die. God's judgement and mercy will rescue both. But the God of whom Robinson speaks cannot do this. Only a God who is transcendent over the world in a very different manner from the God of Robinson's new projection of transcendence, will be able to carry through the work which he has begun.

CHAPTER VI

The Concept of This-Worldly Transcendence and Further Reflections

THE first task of this chapter will be to offer an interpretation and criticism of the work of Gregor Smith, who has written two books that bear on our subject. The first is *The New Man*, published in 1956, and the second, *Secular Christianity*, which followed it in 1966, The second book develops the same themes as the first, and brings into somewhat clearer focus some of the obscurities of the earlier book. Into a general criticism of the two books I shall not try to enter, considering them only in so far as they bear upon our particular theme of divine transcendence.

Much of what is interesting and valuable in *Secular Christianity* is an attempt to expound and expand the thought of Dietrich Bonhoeffer, and what Smith has written on God's transcendence may be read as a commentary on Bonhoeffer's difficult phrase "this-worldly transcendence". In both books Smith is very deeply concerned with the concept of history. The first book starts with a picture of the Old Testament and its portrayal of God as one who encountered his people in the events of their history in the world, meeting them in judgement and mercy. Here there was no dualism between religion and secular life, or between the hope of Israel and the historical future. The faith of the New Testament is massively of the same pattern, Smith claims. It was not until the time of Augustine, and more definitely and rigidly in the time of Thomas Aquinas, that an attempt was made to interpret the Christian faith in terms of Greek metaphysics. The result was a dualism in which the temporal world was contrasted with the eternal one, the supernatural was contrasted with the natural, and the sacred with the secular. The difficulty, Smith tells us, is that once you have separated these two worlds, it is impossible to bring them together again, and the nemesis of such an interpretation is that in the end all reality will be drained from history.

With the coming of the Reformation and the Renaissance, the mediaeval synthesis of nature and supernatural collapsed, and this dualism became incredible. Today there is a fresh understanding of history as the central category for the intrepretation of man's life, and Smith claims that this whole way of looking at things is by no means essentially hostile to the Christian faith, though it will not tolerate the metaphysical dualism into which mediaeval and scholastic thought attempted to translate Christian theology.[1] The reader will recall that in our second chapter we examined Emil Brunner's teaching on divine transcendence to see if it led to such a pernicious dualism, and came to the conclusion that it did not.

Smith indulges in a certain amount of shadow-boxing against the view which he repudiates, and it would have been a help if he had described his opponent a little less vaguely. It is one of his central contentions that the dualism which he repudiates led to a wrong conception of the transcendence of God, who was pictured as dwelling in another world above this world in an eternity which is the negation of time, and whose relation to this world is that of the "wholly-other"[2] and whose action in it is that of a "perpendicular from above". It is this dualism, he claims, which has led the Christian Church away from the world into the worship of a God who can be thought of only in negative terms, and who, as time proceeds, becomes more and more of a ghost without sub-stance.[3]

It is perhaps necessary here to state that the conception of God as the "wholly-other" is not a mark of mediaeval theology, but a polemical conception of Karl Barth, which he employed to warn the Church in a moment of crisis of the dangers of immanentism, and Barth has since, especially in his book *The Humanity of God*, corrected his emphasis.

Smith says, "It is useless to talk of God as the wholly

[1] *The New Man*, p. 42.   [2] *Ibid.*, p. 66.   [3] *Ibid.*, p. 64.

other . . . the importance of the intention behind this assertion is clear, it is the attempt to give God his glory, to preserve his otherness, to indicate his absolute otherness from his creation. But it is meaningless, because any assertion about the wholly other by its own definition excludes any relation or knowledge about what is *wholly* other. The otherness which we meet in God is that otherness which we are able to meet only because he has made himself present to us, has brought himself into relation with us in all the variety of historical situations in which each one of us is set. . . . We believe in him because he has made himself known to us in history, in humanity, in Israel, and especially in the life-situation of one man in the Incarnation."[1]

I am not quite sure against whom this polemic is directed; if it be against Karl Barth, who certainly uses the phrase "wholly other", it would be enough to say that it is a very good representation of his own position, to which therefore he would most cordially assent, with the exception of one or two words which hint at a general revelation, which he repudiates. Karl Barth's central position is surely that the transcendent God has drawn near to us in Christ, and that this gives us the right to speak about him!

With a great many of Gregor Smith's contentions grouped around this theme of God's approach to man in history I would be in the fullest agreement. I think that he is asserting that it is through the events of history that God has revealed himself, and reveals himself and his transcendence, and not in any supramundane world to which we might have access by special philosophical insight or mystical absorption. And faith, in the full sense, can be understood only as man's response to the revelation. If this be what "this-worldly transcendence" means, then I am all for it. In this case Gregor Smith is letting us know that, as a theologian, his primary loyalty is to the revelation made known to faith, and not to any philosophy or natural theology.

Further, Smith, like Bishop Robinson, is not willing to

[1] *The New Man*, p. 66.

surrender faith in God's transcendence. He hopes rather to find a more adequate expression for it. Robinson's attempt to reject the "God out there" is, like Smith's project, an attempt to vindicate God's transcendence for modern man. But here Smith's resemblance to Robinson ends. For Robinson, in the last resort, is rejecting the biblical conception of faith, and adopting a project of natural theology. Smith, on the other hand, is affirming his loyalty to an essentially biblical outlook, and rejecting approaches tinged by natural theology.

It is well to document Smith's determination that transcendence must not be surrendered before we go on to criticise him. He writes, "It is the truth, so simple and yet so hard, that God is not the world. Nor is he man. Between God and the world, betwen God and man . . . there is a gulf which man cannot bridge. . . . In the connexion of faith we need only say here that what has been traditionally called God's transcendence involves a truth which we cannot yield. At the same time, it is a truth which is always in danger of being distorted when taken by itself, or when understood in terms of categories other than those which arise out of the consideration of faith."[1]

Smith than goes on to attempt an interpretation of this transcendence in terms which "arise out of the consideration of faith". These turn out to be historical terms, "God's history with man", or simply, "the history of God". Here we must again affirm our sympathy with his intention to affirm the divine transcendence, and to do so in terms that are not alien to it, and that therefore do not distort our interpretation of it.

At a later point Gregor Smith indicates what he believes to be the true significance of Anselm's ontological proof of the existence of God. This proof, he tells us, is not an attempt to demonstrate to all and sundry the existence of God, starting from the bare idea of God. "His very attempt to think God as real is . . . to be seen as an attempt to grasp transcendence on the basis of that very transcendence which has already entered his life in the historical faith."[2]

I take it for granted that this is what Smith is himself

[1] *Secular Christianity*, p. 21.   [2] *Ibid*, p. 61.

endeavouring to do in these passages on God's transcendence. With this intention I am again in the fullest agreement. Indeed, I could find no better formulation of my own purpose in this book than this, the unfolding of the meaning of the transcendence of God revealed to Christian faith.

Smith's fullest discussion of this theme is to be found in his chapter entitled "An Act of God", of which I shall here attempt a very brief summary. What he is attempting to do is to avoid Scylla and Charybdis. On the one hand, we must not dissipate the reality of God into a number of events or experiences, which would then no longer be *his* actions, or his *actions*. It is the knowledge of the person revealed in the acts which makes them *acts*, and which makes us interpret and understand them as revealing *him*. Scylla is thus the dissipation of God into a series of experiences. Charybdis, the other rock to be avoided, is the conception of God as a static entity existing in a thing-like manner somewhere in an extra-spatial space. This surely is also to be avoided. This is not the way in which to conceive of God's transcendence.

I believe that Gregor Smith intends to say that *in* God's actions God's being, his otherness, his transcendence is revealed to us. We do not only know these actions, but in and through them we know him. He is to be known only in and through them, but he is distinguishable from them. Here Smith uses the analogy of the manner in which other people reveal themselves to us, and are known by us.[1] It is a perfectly legitimate analogy, although it has limitations which Smith goes on to indicate. Our relation to God, he says, is doubly indirect. First, owing to his otherness from us, which is of a different order from the otherness of our human neighbours. And, secondly, owing to the fact that he is known, not to perception and to proof, but to faith. With all this I am in agreement, so that I hope that Professor Smith and I are really fundamentally at one on this crucially important issue.

But, unfortunately, all through this chapter, Smith uses different, and in my opinion, unguarded language, which

[1] *Op. cit.*, p. 119.

does not do justice to God's transcendence. "When we try to speak of God, we believe that he is simply what he does."[1] Here I would rejoin that he is not simply what he does, but the personal being who makes himself known to us through what he does.

Again, Smith writes, "His being is not separable from his action".[2] The intention here is good, but the relation between God's transcendent being and his actions should have been much more guardedly expressed. I cannot have faith in actions, but only in a person. In days like these when there are writers who wish to use the term "God" merely to describe something that happens to them from time to time, we cannot be too careful to distinguish what we are saying from what they say.

Once more, Smith says, speaking of the transcendence of other people whom we encounter, "Transcendence is thus not a reality separate from us, but is the way in which we express the historical reality of encounter with others. . . . In an analogous way, we suggest, we may speak of the relation with God. His transcendence, too, is the expression for the historical reality of his encounter with his creatures. . . . God's being is thus relational through and through. So in this encounter with otherness, while we speak necessarily of dualism, of the one and the other, there is at the same time a fundamental monism: we are all bound up together in the one world, the world of relation. God's otherness is only expressible in terms of his historical being for us."[3]

In this dialectical sparring, it is hard to see who is the enemy. Surely historical encounter with others could not occur unless they were a reality separate from us; much more is the case with God. The relational character of God's being we shall discuss later in detail. But at this point I shall confine myself to saying that certainly God cannot be defined as a being who could never enter into relations, since he has in fact done so. But God is not to be dissolved into his relations. His otherness can be known only through his historical being for us, but

[1] *Ibid.*, p. 117.   [2] *Ibid.*, p. 118.   [3] *Ibid.*, p. 122.

without the otherness, there could be no being for us, and "God" would be dissolved into a mere series of subjective impressions. Gregor Smith's language here is much too imprecise, and his talk of monism, while it may only mean that God is known, or can be known, leaves us with the uncomfortable feeling that Ekkehard is only just round the corner, with his assertion that God is just as dependent on me as I am on him.

Finally, after a paragraph in which he repudiates the two-world metaphysical approach, Smith asks, "Does this mean that we have to abandon the concept of sheer being, as we have abandoned the concept of sheer transcendence? Can we speak of being that lies behind all that we experience in personal encounter? Here, it seems to me, we must again fall back into the trusting silence of negative theology. We cannot speak of God in himself. . . . We cannot put any content into the concept of God's being.'.[1]

Here I would agree with Smith's contention that in speaking of God we must start from the historical revelation in which we believe that we encounter him. But if this is really an encounter with God, it is an encounter with the real God, with God as he is in himself, though there are depths of mystery in God which are beyond our sounding. And further, we do not need to put content into the concept of God's being, for God has himself told us what his being is, holiness, love, and lordship. God has revealed to us his name. If this is not his being, then what is the revelation worth?

Let us think for a moment what is entailed in reflection on that which is given to us in revelaton. Smith is right when he says that God's transcendence is this-worldly, if he means that God's transcendence is revealed in historical acts. It is revealed to men who cannot take a leap, like spiritual flying-fish, out of the ocean of history, and whose categories are therefore taken from the submarine world in which they live, and can be applied only with a conscious inadequacy when they attempt to go beyond the confines of that world. This trans-

[1] *Ibid.*, p. 123. I would agree with Professor Smith if all that he is repudiating is Tillich's *Doctrine of God as Being Itself*, which I also reject (see Chapter IV). But I think he is doing more than this.

cendence is revealed in history, yet it is revealed as transcendence over history. Yet we cannot get outside of history to look at it, as it were, directly.

If we think of God's eternity, we within time can know this in faith, as Brunner says, as God's power[1] over time. Once we try to go beyond this, we are aware, to say the least, of the extreme inadequacy of our thought. The fact is that the relationship of time to eternity is a profound mystery; perhaps indeed the one profound mystery, for it is one aspect of the mystery of God.

Yet it appears that there are certain ways of thinking of eternity which are less inadequate then others. To take one of the most inadequate ways, which indeed must be repudiated, we may try to think of eternity as timeless. But this is a concept which we cannot really form; all that we succeed in thinking of is a moment in which time has stopped, or in which all the moments of time are simultaneous. Such a concept makes time a complete unreality, and drains all blood from freedom and history, as Smith points out.

Another map-projection of eternity is to consider it as flowing alongside of time, and surrounding it. This is terribly inadequate, but what is given us in revelation perhaps necessitates its use. "Before the mountains were brought forth, or ever thou hadst formed the earth and the world, from everlasting to everlasting, Thou art God" (Psalm 95).

It may be that we can go no further than Brunner's conception of God's transcendent eternity as his power over time. Yet faith must surely acknowledge this as a transcendence revealed in history, and also transcendent over history, which yet does not destroy history's reality. Eternity must therefore stand in a positive relationship to time. Deny this transcendence and you are no longer speaking of the self-revealed transcendence of God. So that while revealed in this world, transcendence points beyond it. And this does involve something of a dualism, and if it is a dualism which man cannot ever put together again, then I would say better that than a monism which will not let God be God. The unity of his

---

[1] German *Allmacht*.

world is his affair, and not even the most "grown-up" of
modern men can take such responsibility for the world as to
need to trouble about this. We should remember too, that
what we are attempting here is not a project in natural theology,
but an eristic task, the "unfolding of the meaning of the
transcendence of God revealed to Christian faith".

It may be a disappointment to the readers of this little book
that I have not attempted to come to terms with the thought
of Dietrich Bonhoeffer. There are several reasons for not doing
this. First, when a writer like Gregor Smith is asked whether
we have rightly interpreted what he has written, we have
some hope of receiving an answer, and consequently making
an advance towards clarity and understanding. But Bonhoeffer
cannot "abide our question", and it is notorious that there
are two opposing types of interpretation current. What has
happened is that some theologians have got hold of Bonhoeffer
by the head, and others have got hold of him by the feet, and
they are fighting for possession of the body. Perhaps some day
we may have an authoritative book on what Bonhoeffer
really meant.

Frankly, however, my own opinion is that there are much
more urgent theological tasks than trying to ascertain what
Bonhoeffer meant, and that none would have agreed more
cordially with this estimate than Bonhoeffer himself.

But while we are dealing with Gregor Smith, who has been
so much influenced by Bonhoeffer, it may be worth while
commenting briefly on one statement of the latter, written in
a letter from prison, not meant for publication, from which,
if I understand it, I must dissent.[1] It is evident that here
Bonhoeffer is trying in a brief, telegraphic manner to clarify
a new insight, and has not wholly succeeded. It seems that
he is comparing the notion of God reached by natural theology
with that given us through the revelation in Christ. He
rejects as a false transcendence "an abstract belief in omnipotence, etc.". That, he says, is not a genuine experience
of God, but a partial extension of the world.

[1] *Letters and Papers from Prison*, E.T., p. 179.

His notes then go on to contrast with this the true transcendence. "Encounter with Jesus Christ, implying a complete
orientation of human being in the experience of Jesus as one
whose only concern is for others. This concern of Jesus for
others the experience of transcendence. . . . Faith is participation in this Being of Jesus (incarnation, cross and resurrection).
Our relation to God not a religious relationship to a supreme
Being, absolute in power and goodness, which is a spurious
conception of transcendence but a new life for others, through
participation in the Being of God."

This last telegraphic sentence is the crux; it has been seized
avidly by those who wish to give an account of transcendence
which uses the figure of Christ, without including what might
be called "an I-Thou confrontation" with the transcendent
God. But here the enigmatic phrase "through participation
in the being of God" confronts us and them. All that can be
said here is, that if Bonhoeffer tries to set off "a new life for
others, through participation in the Being of God" against
"a religious relationship to a supreme Being, supreme in
power and goodness"—he is to be repudiated.

Further, we must ask what he means by saying that "the
concern of Jesus for others is the experience of transcendence"?
Does he mean that in this concern of Jesus for others we
experience the transcendence of God? In one sense this is true,
when we see this concern of Jesus as the revelation of the
almighty Father. Then the transcendent God is revealed to
us through Jesus, and we are liberated into faith. But there
are those who know of the concern of Jesus—like van Buren
and Pelz—who do not experience it as the transcendence of
God, for they do not believe in God. So the concern of Jesus is
not just simply the transcendence of God, nor is the knowledge
of it quite simply the knowledge of God's transcendence. To
put the statement philosophically " 'The concern of Jesus is
the transcendence of God' is a synthetic and not an analytical
proposition".

My conclusion is that this tentative note of Bonhoeffer is
itself obscure, and can easily lead to the error of those who

wish to make do without that I-Thou relationship to God the
Father through Christ which is surely the essence of Christian
faith.

A further point which must be made briefly is a protest
againt the bland assumption underlying a good deal of the
new theology, that I can know God only in the encounter
with my human neighbour. The Bible says much about the
intimate connection between knowledge of God and love of
my neighbour. John goes so far as to say that he who claims
to know God and hates his neighbour is a liar. Jesus said that
inasmuch as men were loving and serving their neighbour
they were serving him.

But all this does not imply that we cannot know God or
confront him except in our neighbour. Clearly, our knowledge
of God as Father is mediated, and continues to be mediated,
through the man Jesus Christ. But this is not what the radicals
are claiming. They are setting the "Inasmuch" experience of
the parable of the sheep and the goats in Matthew 25: 31-46
against the practice of prayer. Jesus himself withdrew into
solitude to speak to his Father, and he urged his disciples to
close the door behind them and do the same. It is noticeable
how inadequate the writings of the new radicals are on the
subject of individual prayer. One must sympathise with them
in their reaction against the formality, false conventional
phrasing and unreality of much of our prayer both public and
private. But there is more to it than they find room for, and
it was a true word that Emil Brunner spoke, when he said,
with an eye on the then unfinished theological system of Paul
Tillich, that the acid test of a Christian theology is the account
it is able to give of prayer.[1]

At an earlier stage in this chapter, when criticising Gregor
Smith's description of God's being as relational through and
through, I conceded that God could never be truly defined
as a being who could not enter into relations, since he has in
fact done so. I then undertook to say something at a later point
about his relational character. It is on this very subject that a

[1] *Dogmatik III*, p. 369; E.T., p. 328.

rather serious criticism has been made of Gollwitzer's position by Eberhard Jüngel, another pupil of Karl Barth, and Gollwitzer has himself conceded that Jüngel's criticism has considerable point. Both Gollwitzer and Jüngel are agreed that the task of Christian theology is to interpret faithfully the biblical concept of transcendence, and not to embark on projects of metaphysical or natural theology. But Jüngel points out certain difficulties with which Gollwitzer is embarrassed, and asks whether these are not due to an unconscious injection at one critical point of natural theology, instead of an interpretation of God's being in the biblical sense as Father, Son, and Holy Spirit. This is the central problem discussed in Jüngel's interesting short book *Gottes Sein ist im Werden.*

Put in the shortest form, Jüngel's question is this: In his thoroughly justified assertion about the singularity of God's existence, is Gollwitzer not, at one point at least, in danger of depicting a God for whom revelation and incarnation would be inconceivable? Gollwitzer, for his part, is eager to avoid any dissolution of God into a mere happening within man's consciousness, and he does this by distinguishing between God's existence for himself from his existence for us. Here Gollwitzer claims that his conclusion is implicit in the revelation; this is what God, in his relevation, shows himself to us to be.[1]

But Jüngel suggests that Gollwitzer's particular concept of God's being for himself, at least as described in this important passage, is in fact not of scriptural origin, but is derived from the Aristotelian and Platonic concept of a first substance which from eternity subsists unrelated by itself, being capable of no change. Such a substance, however, could not reveal itself, let alone become incarnate.[2]

Now if, on the other hand, we think of God's transcendence as disclosed in his revelation, we must think of him as the living God. His revelation to us is true, because in it he discloses to us his nature as it is in itself. It is not true to say that from

---

[1] *Existenz Gottes*, p. 175; E.T., p. 175.
[2] *Gottes Sein ist im Werden*, p. 103.

his revelation we deduce its transcendental preconditions, without which it would not be possible. At least it is a much more adequate statement of the truth to say that in his revelation he reveals and interprets to us himself. He is in himself Father, Son and Holy Spirit, and as such his being is act, event, word, for he is continually reaffirming his own existence in this Triune Being. In his revelation he repeats, as it were, to us, what he is in himself.

It has for long been a commonplace of Christian thought that God is love in himself, not merely in relation to his created world. For God is not dependent on his created world; it is wholly dependent on him. But the love which unites the modes of being within the Trinity is the love which moved forth freely to create, bless, and save the world in Christ. And this, I would submit, is the truth behind the statement that God's being is relational through and through. God shows himself in his revelation to be a God whose very being is being in act, he is not inert substance. And since he does reveal himself in history, we must say also that in a sense his own being is in itself also historical—though we cannot know directly or precisely what we mean by the words "in a sense". All that we can say is that while the word "historical" does not mean the same in both cases, there is an analogy between the two senses. In other words, there is a relation between God's time and our time which is not purely negative, but in a mysterious sense positive. It is as such a one that God reveals himself, as the God who "from eternity" elected to create man, and to become one with man in the person of the incarnate logos, and to unite man with himself in blessedness. Objections raised on the grounds of natural theology or philosophy that God cannot reveal himself, cannot become incarnate, are to be rejected. Who are we to lay down conditions to God on the basis of our natural theology?

I am aware of the dizzy altitudes in which we have been moving, and of the feeling which the reader may have that this is surely an incursion into a metaphysical world to which we have no legitimate access. But I would again submit that the statements to which we have been led arise from an interpretation of God's transcendence in history as seen by faith. And that the God who there reveals himself to us, does so in such a way that we are forced in the end to say certain things about him which are right on the verge of permissible utterance. Yet we feel that we must say them, though saying them our words and our understanding falter and stop.

At a much earlier stage in this study the question was proposed—"What does the transcendence of God mean as the Bible understands it?" There we thought of the concepts of God's name, his lordship, his character as creator, his right-eousness and holy love. These qualities together made up the *content* of the divine transcendence. But light is to be obtained also from the *forms* in which that transcendence is revealed in the Bible. In the concluding pages something must be said about two of these forms, God's mighty works, and his word.

These two concepts are interwoven through the whole biblical narrative. One of the first of the mighty works is God's covenant with his people. This is first and foremost a mighty work—what greater work could there be than that the Lord and the Creator of all should approach a family of men in the fleeting years of their history, and take them into a special relationship with himself? But the covenant is also a word spoken, a promise made, and God's word, spoken to his people through the prophets, goes on interpreting the meaning of the covenant in the varying events of the history that succeeded the making of it.

There are other mighty works that followed, deliverances of Israel, and judgements on Israel and the surrounding peoples, and God's word followed these, and sometimes preceded them, helping God's people to see that they *were* his acts, and what his meaning and purpose in them was.

God's word, pointing his people towards events which were going to happen, could have the force of a threat, but much more often of a promise. The reference of the word is always both backwards and forwards in time; perhaps the favourite manner in which God speaks to his people is to remind them of his mighty acts in the past, to reason with them that since these things are so, they should not only be grateful, but should trust him for the unknown future. Werner Pelz has put this beautifully. "The people of Jahweh are encouraged to hope in him because he was and is the awakener of their hopes, to trust in him because he has vindicted his trustworthiness. . . . Jahweh's forgiveness is his persistent calling and recalling into hope and trust and love".[1]

Now this concept of the word is of great interest in our study of God's transcendence. It is *spoken*, and this very character is a sign of sovereign initiative of God's part, his grace, his search for communion with me. Words in general are a means of initiating communion, which at the same time separate the speaker from the one addressed, yet also unite them in such a manner that there is no fusion. The bond which is created by the word is by no means purely an intellectual one; it can be a supreme means of self-communication. The concept of the word as used in the Bible is a guarantee of God's transcendence inasmuch as it is a word of grace; it calls for a humble response of gratitude, while as a word of command it calls for a response of faith and obedience. Here we are not allowed to remain spectators, God affirms his transcendence[2] by calling for our free yet obedient response.

The Bible sometimes, though more rarely, uses another image, that of vision. God appeared to Isaiah in the Temple:[3] Christ appeared transfigured to the disciples.[4] The danger of vision is that men would wish to linger at the point where it was given, "Master, it is good for us to be here, and let us build three tabernacles"[5]. The concept of sight is perhaps less appropriate to our existence as travellers through time than the concept of hearing. For sight belongs essentially to the end of

---

[1] *God is no More*, p. 114.
[2] I have not here drawn attention to the very important difference between the revelation of the Old Testament and that of the New. In the Old Testament Christ, who is himself the Word, is still to come; in the New Testament he has already come. But this does not mean, as Altizer claims, that with the incarnation God has in any way lost his transcendence.
[3] Isaiah 6.   [4] Mark 9:2-8.   [5] Mark 9:5.

the journey, when the pure in heart will see God. It does not therefore call us forth into the future as does the word, whose true correlative in man is hearing, and faith and obedient trust. God calls to his people, summoning them forth into the future in faith.

Yet this faith is not irrational, There is an intellectual element in our apprehension of the word. And it does not only demand our understanding, but God also reasons with his people. The faith he demands is reasonable, for, having done great works, and having in his word interpreted them, he challenges his people on the strength of their experience of him in the past to trust him for the unknown future. And there he promises to meet them as the one who will be what he will be,[1] the God who remains Lord, but a Lord of infinite promise and blessing.

In this context Gollwitzer has written a fine passage indicating the special type of rationality that belongs to faith. He writes, "Is it really so? Has the world, or have we, a Lord, this Lord? . . . This is the question posed by doubt. It cannot be answered by proofs from the external world. But it must not be discredited as if the believer had to shake himself free of such a question, and must understand his faith as a pure decision, that is, a resolve that could be given assurance by no objective reality—a resolve to live as the hearer of such a word. . . . Grace cannot be a postulate . . . (the believer) is promised that the one whom here he is permitted to hear will stand by his word, and prove to him that it really is so."[2]

Thus while we cannot think of allocating the transcendent God a place wholly within the logically coherent structure of our own experience, and so demonstrating to ourselves and to others that he exists, yet we can believe that his truth will vindicate itself in his own way, that he will be true to himself, to his own declared purposes, and to his promises to us. This is the meaning of faith. Here then, with a reference to the title of one of Emil Brunner's books *Truth as Encounter*—the truth that came and comes through Christ, we approach the end of

[1] Exodus 3:14.   [2] *Existenz Gottes*, pp. 173-4; E.T., p. 215.

our study. As Brunner pointed out, the word of God came to the prophets, and was different from them,The word did not need to come to Jesus, he himself is the word. And his person is also the greatest of God's mighty works, God with us, Immanuel. At this point, in his incarnation, cross and resurrection, there is given the culminating revelation of the transcendence of God.

CHAPTER VII

Recapitulation and Conclusions

THE time has now come to recapitulate our argument, and draw its threads together. We started with the observation that the trend of modern theological discussion shows how necessary it is to re-examine the notion of God's transcendence. Some writers, like J. A. T. Robinson, are claiming that a very radical restatement of the concept is needed, while others, belonging to the "God is dead" school, are prepared to sponsor a type of Christianity that discards altogether the thought of a transcendent God. The shock of these events has focussed attention on the subject. On all sides people are asking the question "What does God's transcendence really mean? Can we in any sense still speak of 'God up there'?—or if not, of 'God out there'? Or is God 'the depth of being'?" My aim in this book has been to give some kind of answer to these questions, and I have mentioned the discussions of other writers mainly with a view to developing and clarifiying my own position.

There is a divergence of opinion not only about the meaning of transcendence, but also with regard to the historical causes of the present predicament. Leaving on one side acknowledged cultural phenomena such as the prestige of science, and the apparent self-sufficiency of a positivistic outlook on life, opinions differ radically as to the theological causes of the present difficult situation. Some maintain that it is due to too much natural theology, and others that it is due to too little. Leaving this issue undecided for the moment, I go on in the second chapter to speak of that transcendence of God which is central to the Biblical revelation, taking it as source and norm of our thinking, and trying to clarify its implications for our thought today.

Early in the second chapter I indicate that the transcendent

God must be regarded by Christians as the supreme reality, and that this demands a continuing engagement and encounter with other thinkers, not only with those who deny the reality of God, or are in danger of involuntarily compromising it, but also with those whose specific interest lies in special fields, for example, in ethics, in sociology and psychology, and in other disciplines which study the various activities and powers of man. In such discussions it becomes apparent that other concepts must be used than those to be found in the Bible. But I urge that the important thing is not what concepts we use, but where our chief loyalty is to be placed, whether in the revelation to which the Bible bears witness, or in some philosophy or natural theology by which the Biblical revelation is to be judged, and according to whose norms it must, if necessary, be reinterpreted. By so doing I declare myself as against those who seek to cure the illness of modern theological uncertainty by a fresh injection of natural theology. Yet I believe that their real concern and interest is legitimate. They wish for a fresh and vigorous engagement with secular thought, which indeed has been too long delayed. In later discussions of the contributions of other writers, I make it my business to ask in each case—what does this man regard as his ultimate loyalty, the biblical revelation, or some other authority?

The main theme of the second chapter is, however, the attempt to expound the biblical understanding of divine transcendence, taking as a guiding line the thought of Emil Brunner, which in my opinion offers a short and generally reliable account of the biblical understanding. Here God is pictured as the one who reveals, by a free act of grace, his name and his nature to men who could not have known him apart from his revelation.

God is Lord, he is holy, he is love, and his love and his transcendence are supremely expressed in his freedom from his own law, and his forgiveness of sinners, winning them over to responsive love without infringing their freedom. Such is God's nature, but there are attributes of God which describe him not as he is in his nature, but as he shows himself to be in relation to the created world. His power and his eternity are expressions of his rule over the world, and his sovereignty over time, which are both created magnitudes. Attempts to describe these attributes as directly applicable to his nature are apt to lead to views that leave no room for human freedom, and empty time of reality. There are difficulties about Brunner's teaching here, but it seems not open to criticisms made by contemporary theologians that hitherto accepted views of divine transcendence necessarily create a disastrous dualism between a transcendent world and the world of human history, which latter is inevitably drained of reality and significance.

The third chapter goes on to claim that while God's transcendence is primarily disclosed in the historical revelation to which the Bible bears witness, in the light of that revelation Christian faith must claim that the transcendence of God is also revealed in creation and general human experience, though rightly understood and interpreted only in the light of Christian faith. There is thus no place in human life where God has left himself without a witness. In response to this revelation in creation there are two responses among men, inextricably intermingled. There is the response of a search and a longing for God, and the response of a flight from him. To all this the Bible bears a unanimous witness, and the belief that there is this revelation and this ambiguous response is an integral part of Christian theology. It is also in the long run necessary for Christian faith to maintain that man is essentially a responsive, responsible being, standing in continual confrontation with God, and however he may misinterpret this confrontation by idolatry, or close his eyes to it in blindness, he is unable to escape from it, for it is a component of his humanity. This doctrine of the divine transcendence is linked up with the doctrine of the image of God in man, and certain statements by exponents of the new radical theology are in danger of denying both.

I claim accordingly that the transcendence of God is encountered first, (and supremely) in the biblical revelation, and also in the wider experience of men in the general revelation. In neither case is it, however, a datum which is public as is the world of sense-perception. It exists rather in the form of a continual divine self-giving and a claim continually renewed, in which the sovereign God remains man's master and Lord, and never puts himself under human control. It is in this sense that I describe the transcendence of God as something belonging to experience, and given in experience.

There are, however, various attempts to bring this transcendence within the pattern of an already existent philosophy, and thus to domesticate it, to make it, perhaps, the copestone of a philosophical system, or to reinterpret it in the terms which a particular philosophical system will permit. But when this is done, the transcendent loses its over-againstness, God's transcendence is no longer that which encounters man from beyond, and which must be responded to with reverence and gratitude, but is a word which we can speak to ourselves. What happens then is that the true transcendence which was experienced in the special or the general revelation, is lost, and a false transcendence is created by the misinterpretation.

It seems to me that in different ways this is what happens in the theologies of Tillich and of Robinson, which are discussed in the fourth and fifth chapters. There I have tried to show that we do not have that direct access to being by which Tillich claims to evaluate the symbolical knowledge given to us in revelation, and I have endeavoured to demonstrate that Robinson's attempt to form a new projection of transcendence (depth-of-being rather than God-out-there) collapses because it can be made to appear solvent only by illegitimate loans from the God-out-there theology which it claims to replace.

Finally, after drawing attention once more to the content of God's revealed transcendence as God's name, his Lordship, his righteousness and his holy love, I have suggested that much may be learnt from two forms in which the Bible gives expression to that transcendence—God's word and his mighty acts. In both, his sovereignty and initiative are preserved, as is also his desire to create communion and to save. The God who speaks and who does mighty acts remains irreducibly over against us as the living God. Yet, though he cannot be made the coping-stone of a human system, there is a rationality about his transcendence, and in the faith to which he summons us. For God appeals to his revelation in the past as a ground for our obedience and trust in the future.

APPENDIX A

Edward Farley on the Transcendence of God

DR. FARLEY takes the view that there are two approaches to the theme of transcendence, and two transcendents, the metaphysical and the kerygmatic. The first is the most real being studied by metaphysical philosophy, and the second is the God who discloses himself in the Christian revelation. The nature of the relationship between these two transcendents is one of the most baffling problems for the philosophical theologian, and the situation reached at the moment is best described as an impasse.

So much is laid down in the introductory chapter,[1] and the main body of the book is an able study of the thought of a number of contemporary philosophical theologians. Then in the last chapter the author reverts to his central problems, which he formulates for us as follows:

"When we consider transcendence, the question becomes, What can be said about the Transcendent on the basis of human capabilities, or, in older language, on the basis of a *theologia naturalis*? Does human experience in and of itself arrive at a Transcendent? If so, what is its nature? Or, on the other side, What can be said about the Transcendent on the basis of the Transcendent's revelation of itself? The purpose of this chapter is to isolate these two questions, in so far as they can be isolated, and then pose the problem of their relationship, hoping thus to find a way to at least gaze beyond the impasse, even if we fail to resolve it."[2]

The chapter proceeds with a section on the Transcendent as Limit and then follows a section on the Transcendent as God. The first of these sections is written about the philosophical transcendent, which appears to be seen by natural theology in four modes—the Beginning, the End, the Depth, and the Height. Yet when we look further into the argument, we find that what we are offered is not any content of knowledge, but four unanswered questions. What this section really

---

[1] *The Transcendence of God.*   [2] *Ibid.*, p. 193.

shows to us is merely the fact that all our knowledge is confined to a tiny illuminated area in the midst of darkness and mystery. We have an urge to seek the beginning and the end, to know the mysterious depth underlying the realities which confront us in the known, and to have knowledge of the Other that encounters us. But "even as man is not the Depth, neither is he the Height, nor does he enter or possess the Height. He may wonder about, worship, or try to avoid, the Height, all of which are signs that when man would enter the Height by way of his ever-growing and ever-collapsing towers of Babel, he finds only the dark".[1]

But surely we must object that to call this limit the Transcendent is not to give it any tangible unity—it is just another word for the mystery that our knowledge is limited. If this be the case, then the transcendent of metaphysics, seen as it were from below, is nothing more then a series of unanswered questions, and the problem of its relation to the kerygmatic transcendence of the special revelation hardly arises, unless we are to believe that the latter may provide in some way answers to these questions.

When we pass on to Dr. Farley's next section, "The Transcendent as God", we find first a preliminary passage in which the author deals with the epistemological question, i.e. with the question how God is known in revelation; the answer being given, that he is known through grace, by God's giving himself to be known in Christ.

Then follow four sections in which the ontological question is raised and answered, God gives himself to be known as the transcendent creator, as the fulfiller, as the preserver, and as the Holy One. Here Farley and the present writer would be in substantial agreement.[2]

It will be noted that here we have a correlation of the four kerygmatic answers with the four questions of natural theology which at once makes us ask whether what we have here is not a Tillichian type of theology, with the disadvantages that we saw above in the chapter on Tillich. But as Farley points out, the questions here are not dictated by a particular world-view,[3] as in Tillich's theology; further, the answers actually do not

[1] *Ibid.*, p. 201.
[2] See Chapter II.
[3] *The Transcendence of God*, p. 201.

directly respond to the questions, but transform them in answering them[1]; and, lastly, I strongly suspect that the four questions were formulated with a view to fitting the kerygmatic answers, so that the gospel is not here, in Hamilton's telling phrase, "put in the power of an inquisitor"[2] as in Tillich's theology.

At this point I would wish to set forth my own different position, and make it clearer by contrasting it with Farley's. I do not accept his fundamental pattern, which involves the setting forth of a philosophical transcendence over against a kerygmatic one, the two being, as it were, equal partners and competitors. For my thought the governing pattern is rather that of a transcendence experientially revealed in encounter, whether in the special revelation or in the general one. Natural theology in my opinion inevitably destroys the transcendence revealed in the general revelation. For natural theology inevitably tries to fit in the transcendent within the coherent structure of our thinking, and to "place" it, to bring the mind to rest by including it within the monologue of our thought. Therefore, what is said of the transcendent on the basis of a natural theology will not reach the true transcendent, but a false one, or else at some point, probably the last step of the argument, there will be, not a step in the chain of logical reasoning, but a leap, and a false identification of that which has been inferred with the true transcendent known to faith. This is what happens in Aquinas's five proofs of the existence of God, with the repeated conclusion in each case "and this we call God".[3] The true transcendent is not anti-rational, but is met with only in the form of encounter, whether it be in the general or in the special revelation.

It seems to me that after talking of the transcendent reached by natural theology, Farley is forced to concede that nothing is reached, but that questions are asked without certain answers being heard, and that even to give the limits which surround us the name of "the Encompassing" (*Das Umgreifende*) is to posit an entity which natural theology cannot legitimately substantialize. Yet, speaking from the viewpoint of faith, I

---

[1] *Ibid.*, p. 211.
[2] *The System and the Gospel*, p. 121.
[3] *Summa Thelogiae*, I, 2, 3. *Utrum Deus Sit.*

would feel justified in saying that that which encounters us in the general revelation is God. What natural theology does is to remove that element of encounter, and by so doing it misses the true transcendence, and creates a false one.

APPENDIX B

The Radical Theology's Interpretation of John 14:9

"HE that hath seen me hath seen the Father." It is interesting to note that the Christologies of Pelz and van Buren rest almost entirely upon this verse, and, further, on what must be called a deliberate misunderstanding of it.

They ignore, not only the unanimous teaching of the New Testament, but also the fact that when Jesus said these words, he was speaking to men who shared with him the whole tradition of the Old Testament, for whom, therefore "the heavens were not empty" but who had from infancy been brought up in the knowledge of the God, whom he revealed more profoundly to them as Father.

In his article in *Theology* (LVIII, 1964, p. 343 ff.), Mr. Don Cupitt says that the Gospel has always been assumed to deal with both Christ and the Father and that "this implies that we have some knowledge of God before the Gospel", "and so, if we say that Jesus is from God, manifests God, or is God, we are making a synthetic assertion"—not merely analysing the content of the concept 'Jesus' ". With both these statements I would heartily agree. But this does not imply, as a logical consequence, the belief in a valid natural theology, as Mascall and Cupitt seem to assume. It does imply that the God whom Jesus reveals is not Jesus himself, but a transcendent Power other than him, though identical with him in holiness and love. But to know of this God, or about him, it is not necessary to posit a valid natural theology, but at the most a general revelation. Mascall can hardly be blamed for confusing the two, when Karl Barth, whom he is criticizing, has shown himself quite incapable of distinguishing them.

There remains however the case of the man who passes straight from atheism to Christian faith, a transition which would be inexplicable on Mascall's presuppositions. To account for such conversions can we not say that the figure of Jesus, his words and actions, portrayed in the gospels, may produce such an impact on the reader, that the latter makes the leap of faith, saying to himself, "If *this* man said that there was a God who was his Father, then I am impelled to take him at his word"?

It must be pointed out, further, that *pace* van Buren, Pelz and Körner,[1] Jesus' witness to himself in the gospels is always strictly subordinate to his witness to the Father. One might even say that in the Fourth Gospel, where Jesus' claims for himself are far more openly made than in the Synoptics, his subordination to the Father is correspondingly more emphasized. In short, the Jesus of Pelz, van Buren, and Körner, who merely draws attention to himself, is an even more naïve product of twentieth century positivism than the nineteenth century Jesus was of the contemporary liberal humanism, whose representatives Albert Schweitzer described as looking into the deep well of history and seeing there only the reflection of their own faces.

[1] Johannes Körner, "Die transzendente Wirklichkeit Gottes" (*Zeitschrift für Theologie und Kirche*, December 1966).